# SEPTEMBER MORNING

## TEN YEARS OF POEMS AND READINGS FROM THE 9/11 CEREMONIES
### NEW YORK CITY

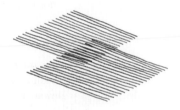

Compiled and Edited by Sara Lukinson

. . . . . . . . . . . . . . . . . . . . . . . . . . . .

Foreword by Michael R. Bloomberg
Mayor of the City of New York
Chair of the National September 11 Memorial & Museum

. . . . . . . . . . . . . . . . . . . . . . . . . . . .

powerHouse Books
Brooklyn, New York

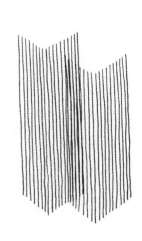

**Foreword by Mayor Bloomberg** One year after the terrorist attacks of September 11, 2001, our city faced a daunting challenge: hosting a commemoration that was worthy of the memories of those who perished and that offered consolation to family members still mourning the loss of their loved ones. The world would be watching, as so many looked to New York City to remember and reflect on a day that brought unspeakable sadness but also unsurpassed heroics.

This book represents the efforts to create a program that paid tribute to both the national tragedy and great personal grief. The passages are some of the most moving poems, letters, song lyrics, and excerpts from literary and historical works ever gathered. Their words reflect sorrow, but also our resolve to go on, together.

When we began planning our commemoration, we knew that we needed to return to the site of the attacks. Months of recovery and cleanup efforts had cleared the World Trade Center site of rubble, leaving behind only bedrock – the hallowed ground on which we would remember and rebuild.

The plan was to stand together as one and to honor each and every person we lost. In recognition of each individual life and the loved ones left behind, every victim's name was to be read aloud. There was a simple dignity to this approach, and it proved both poignant and inspiring.

Over the past ten years, thousands have come to the ceremonies to read the names. And in listening to those names, we have heard an unspoken story about the World Trade Center: how it brought people together from every race and religion, every culture and country. Family members were joined in the reading of the names by others – including first responders, volunteers, and construction workers – who shared in the loss and recovery efforts.

At every commemoration, family members were asked to speak about their loved ones. With each short speech, a portrait of the men and women who worked and died at the World Trade Center began to emerge. We heard about engineers, pastry chefs, police officers, traders, flight attendants, firefighters – and people in many other professions. Family members told stories about loving fathers, daughters, wives, brothers, and sisters. These personally written pieces helped bring to life the names being read.

To keep the focus on the victims and their families, it was important to us to keep contemporary political rhetoric out of the commemoration. Instead, the program invoked some of the great words from literature and our nation's history. In that first year we quoted Abraham Lincoln's Gettysburg Address, reminding listeners that our nation had withstood heartbreak before, and that once again we would "highly resolve that these dead shall not have died in vain – that this nation, under God, shall have a new birth of freedom – and that government of the people, by the people, for the people, shall not perish from the earth." The American spirit of freedom would always be the foundation of this site.

In each succeeding year, readings were chosen to represent different family members' points of view and their personal perspectives of the tragedy. These subjects became the guide in choosing the readings from a wide range of sources and styles, periods and places. They speak of love and loss, remembrance and celebration, courage, compassion, the gentle encouragement to go on, and the rebuilding itself.

There are, of course, elements of the ceremony that cannot be captured in a book, including the music. The mournful sounds of the bagpipes, traditionally played at funerals for firefighters and police officers, would each year signal the beginning of the ceremony. And throughout the entire reading of the names, classical music was performed by small ensembles and chamber groups from all over the city. One by one, each group quietly took their turn on the stage, rotating throughout the ceremonies and accompanying the readers as they recited at the podium. Children's choirs opened and closed the ceremonies, and as the years went on, noted soloists were asked to sing midway through the tributes. The choice of songs was made as carefully as the choice of readings. The day ended with trumpets playing "Taps."

One more element was added to the ceremony that you cannot hear in this book: the moments of silence. It is a time-honored tradition, in all ceremonies marking a moment of national import, to observe a moment of silence. At the ceremonies, we would stop to mark moments of impact and collapse as we turned our hearts and minds to those terrifying and tragic minutes in our nation's history.

In 2011, on the tenth anniversary of the attacks, the National September 11 Memorial was unveiled. On this meaningful day, we drew upon passages read in previous years to provide a sense of reflection on the past decade as we revealed the Memorial and turned with hope toward the future. At last, the gaping hole where the ceremonies had begun was now rebuilt into an everlasting tribute to all those who perished. The 9/11 Memorial, which includes two beautiful waterfalls in the footprints of each tower, now forever proclaims the names that were read aloud each year, engraved in bronze along the edges of each pool.

While we worked toward creating a lasting memorial that would honor the victims of September 11, our hope was to create a ceremony that was strong and simple and spoke across time, cultures, religions, and backgrounds. The answer to the violence of the attacks would be the humanity of our voices and the kindness we showed to one another. This book is a testament to those ceremonies and the efforts over the past ten years to remember and reflect upon that September morning that changed us forever.

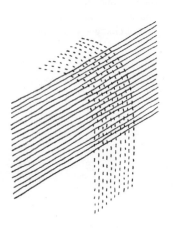

2002

**THE FIRST YEAR**


2003

**THE LOSS OF A PARENT**


2004

**THE LOSS OF A CHILD**


2005

**THE LOSS OF A SIBLING**


2006

**THE LOSS OF A SPOUSE OR PARTNER**


2007

**FIRST RESPONDERS**


2008

**THE INTERNATIONAL FAMILY**


2009

**A DAY OF SERVICE**


2010

**REBUILDING**


2011

**THE TENTH ANNIVERSARY**

. . . . . . . . . . . . . . .


**ACKNOWLEDGMENTS**

2002
**THE FIRST YEAR**

INTRODUCTION

Again, today, we are a nation who mourns.
Again, today, we take into our hearts and minds those who perished on this
site one year ago; and those who came to toil in the rubble to bring order out of
chaos, and those who throughout these last 12 months have struggled to help
us make sense of our despair.

Now, we join with all our fellow Americans in a minute of silence, led by
President Bush from the South Lawn of the White House in Washington, DC.

..............................

One hundred thirty-nine years ago, President Abraham Lincoln looked out at
his wounded nation, as he stood on a once beautiful field that had become its
saddest and largest burying ground. Then, it was Gettysburg. Today, it is the
World Trade Center, where we gather on native soil to share our common grief.

LINCOLN'S GETTYSBURG ADDRESS

FOUR SCORE AND SEVEN YEARS AGO OUR FATHERS BROUGHT FORTH ON THIS
CONTINENT, A NEW NATION, CONCEIVED IN LIBERTY, AND DEDICATED TO THE
PROPOSITION THAT ALL MEN ARE CREATED EQUAL.

NOW WE ARE ENGAGED IN A GREAT CIVIL WAR, TESTING WHETHER THAT NATION,
OR ANY NATION SO CONCEIVED AND SO DEDICATED, CAN LONG ENDURE. WE ARE
MET ON A GREAT BATTLE-FIELD OF THAT WAR. WE HAVE COME TO DEDICATE A
PORTION OF THAT FIELD, AS A FINAL RESTING PLACE FOR THOSE WHO HERE GAVE
THEIR LIVES THAT THAT NATION MIGHT LIVE. IT IS ALTOGETHER FITTING AND
PROPER THAT WE SHOULD DO THIS.

BUT, IN A LARGER SENSE, WE CAN NOT DEDICATE — WE CAN NOT CONSECRATE —
WE CAN NOT HALLOW — THIS GROUND. THE BRAVE MEN, LIVING AND DEAD, WHO
STRUGGLED HERE, HAVE CONSECRATED IT, FAR ABOVE OUR POOR POWER TO
ADD OR DETRACT. THE WORLD WILL LITTLE NOTE, NOR LONG REMEMBER WHAT WE
SAY HERE, BUT IT CAN NEVER FORGET WHAT THEY DID HERE. IT IS FOR US THE
LIVING, RATHER, TO BE DEDICATED HERE TO THE UNFINISHED WORK WHICH THEY
WHO FOUGHT HERE HAVE THUS FAR SO NOBLY ADVANCED.

IT IS RATHER FOR US TO BE HERE DEDICATED TO THE GREAT TASK REMAINING
BEFORE US — THAT FROM THESE HONORED DEAD WE TAKE INCREASED DEVOTION
TO THAT CAUSE FOR WHICH THEY GAVE THE LAST FULL MEASURE OF DEVOTION —
THAT WE HERE HIGHLY RESOLVE THAT THESE DEAD SHALL NOT HAVE DIED IN
VAIN — THAT THIS NATION, UNDER GOD, SHALL HAVE A NEW BIRTH OF FREEDOM
— AND THAT THIS GOVERNMENT OF THE PEOPLE, BY THE PEOPLE, FOR
THE PEOPLE, SHALL NOT PERISH FROM THIS EARTH.

READING OF THE NAMES

They were our neighbors, our husbands, our children, our sisters, our brothers, and our wives. Our countrymen, and our friends.
They were us.

YOU WERE THE BEST FATHER

My stepfather, Franco Lalama, was an engineer for the Port Authority. He worked on the 64th floor of the World Trade Center. I read this for his memorial.

I don't remember the last time I told him that I loved him. I would give anything to go back to the morning of September 11 and tell him how much I appreciate everything he's done for me. But I think he knows that now. In my eyes, he died a hero, and how much more could you ask for.

There's a quote that pretty much speaks for itself:

YOU NEVER LOSE ANYTHING. NOT REALLY. THINGS, PEOPLE — THEY GO AWAY, SOONER OR LATER. YOU CAN'T HOLD THEM ANYMORE THAN YOU CAN HOLD THE MOONLIGHT. BUT IF THEY'VE TOUCHED YOU, IF THEY'RE INSIDE OF YOU, THEN THEY'RE STILL YOURS.

Frank, as I look back on these days, I realize how much I'll truly miss you and how much I truly love you. You were the best father I could ask for. I miss you. And I hope you didn't hurt too much.

Love, Marianne

I CAN HEAR MY DADDY SAY

My father, Keefe, was a chef on the 96th floor of the World Trade Center. This poem made me feel like my daddy was speaking to me.

I GIVE YOU THIS ONE THOUGHT TO KEEP —
I AM WITH YOU STILL — I DO NOT SLEEP.
I AM A THOUSAND WINDS THAT BLOW.
I AM THE DIAMOND GLINTS ON SNOW,
I AM THE SUNLIGHT ON RIPENED GRAIN,
I AM THE GENTLE AUTUMN RAIN.
WHEN YOU AWAKEN IN THE MORNING'S HUSH
I AM THE SWIFT, UPLIFTING RUSH
OF QUIET BIRDS IN CIRCLED FLIGHT.
I AM THE SOFT STARS THAT SHINE AT NIGHT.
DO NOT THINK OF ME AS GONE —
I AM WITH YOU STILL — IN EACH NEW DAWN.

Brittany Clark

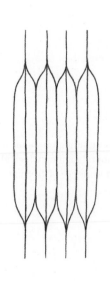

THE GROUND WE STAND ON

One year ago, the ground we are standing on shook, and the earth gave way.
Although the buildings fell, the foundation on which all Americans stand
will never fall, for it is the sacred principle of freedom and equality on which
we build our lives.

THE DECLARATION OF INDEPENDENCE (excerpt)

WE HOLD THESE TRUTHS TO BE SELF-EVIDENT, THAT ALL MEN ARE CREATED EQUAL, THAT THEY ARE ENDOWED BY THEIR CREATOR WITH CERTAIN UNALIENABLE RIGHTS, THAT AMONG THESE ARE LIFE, LIBERTY AND THE PURSUIT OF HAPPINESS. THAT TO SECURE THESE RIGHTS, GOVERNMENTS ARE INSTITUTED AMONG MEN, DERIVING THEIR JUST POWERS FROM THE CONSENT OF THE GOVERNED...

AND FOR THE SUPPORT OF THIS DECLARATION, WITH A FIRM RELIANCE ON THE PROTECTION OF DIVINE PROVIDENCE, WE MUTUALLY PLEDGE TO EACH OTHER OUR LIVES, OUR FORTUNES, AND OUR SACRED HONOR.

2003
**THE LOSS OF A PARENT**

INTRODUCTION

Today, again, we are a city that mourns.

We come here to honor those we lost and to remember this date with sorrow, but we also remember with pride. And from that comes our resolve to go forward, our faces and hopes turned toward the light.

In keeping with this, the children of our city and the children who lost loved ones will lead our ceremonies. It is in them that the spirit of New York lives, carrying both our deepest memories and the bright promise of tomorrow.

At this time, please join us and all New Yorkers for a moment of silence.

**Mayor Bloomberg**

HE WORKED ON THE 88TH FLOOR

My father, Pete Negron, worked on the 88th floor of the World Trade Center. I wanted to read you this poem because it says what I was feeling.

STARS

I LIKED THE WAY THEY LOOKED DOWN FROM THE SKY
AND DIDN'T SEEM TO MIND THE WAY I CRIED.

AND DIDN'T SAY, "NOW WIPE AWAY THOSE TEARS,"
OR, "TELL US, TELL US WHAT'S THE MATTER HERE!"

BUT SHINING THROUGH THE DARK THEY CALMLY STAYED,
AND GENTLY HELD ME IN THEIR QUIET WAY.

I FELT THEM WATCHING OVER ME, EACH ONE —
AND LET ME CRY AND CRY TILL I WAS DONE.

Peter Negron

READING OF THE NAMES

Last year America's Poet Laureate, Billy Collins, wrote a poem he called "The Names" about the 2,792 who perished that day. Here are its closing lines:

NAMES ETCHED ON THE HEAD OF A PIN.

ONE NAME SPANNING A BRIDGE, ANOTHER UNDERGOING A TUNNEL.

A BLUE NAME NEEDLED INTO THE SKIN.

NAMES OF CITIZENS, WORKERS, MOTHERS AND FATHERS,

THE BRIGHT-EYED DAUGHTER, THE QUICK SON.

ALPHABET OF NAMES IN A GREEN FIELD.

NAMES IN THE SMALL TRACKS OF BIRDS.

NAMES LIFTED FROM A HAT

OR BALANCED ON THE TIP OF THE TONGUE.

NAMES WHEELED INTO THE DIM WAREHOUSE OF MEMORY.

SO MANY NAMES, THERE IS BARELY ROOM ON THE WALLS OF THE HEART.

Mayor Bloomberg

I THINK CONTINUALLY OF THOSE WHO WERE TRULY GREAT (excerpt)

I'd like to read these lines from a poem by Stephen Spender:

I THINK CONTINUALLY OF THOSE WHO WERE TRULY GREAT.
WHO, FROM THE WOMB, REMEMBERED THE SOUL'S HISTORY
THROUGH CORRIDORS OF LIGHT WHERE THE HOURS ARE SUNS
ENDLESS AND SINGING. WHOSE LOVELY AMBITION
WAS THAT THEIR LIPS, STILL TOUCHED WITH FIRE,
SHOULD TELL OF THE SPIRIT CLOTHED FROM HEAD TO FOOT IN SONG.
AND WHO HOARDED FROM THE SPRING BRANCHES
THE DESIRES FALLING ACROSS THEIR BODIES LIKE BLOSSOMS.

. . .

SEE HOW THESE NAMES ARE FÊTED BY THE WAVING GRASS
AND BY THE STREAMERS OF WHITE CLOUD
AND WHISPERS OF WIND IN THE LISTENING SKY.
THE NAMES OF THOSE WHO IN THEIR LIVES FOUGHT FOR LIFE
WHO WORE AT THEIR HEARTS THE FIRE'S CENTER.
BORN OF THE SUN THEY TRAVELED A SHORT WHILE TOWARDS THE SUN,
AND LEFT THE VIVID AIR SIGNED WITH THEIR HONOR.

Governor Pataki

LITTLE BOY OF MINE

My son, Carl, was a firefighter with Ladder 2 in midtown Manhattan.
I wrote this poem for my son. Everyone who was killed that day was someone's
son or daughter.

IN THE QUIET OF MY HEART
I HOLD YOUR HAND
LITTLE BOY OF MINE.

I HEAR THE GIGGLE OF YOUR LAUGH
AND I SEE THE SMILE IN YOUR EYES.
I WATCH YOU GROW
AND OF YOUR FUTURE DREAM.
I WANT ALL YOUR DREAMS FOR YOU.

I WANT ALWAYS TO BE THERE
TO HELP IN ANY WAY.
TO ALWAYS MAKE THINGS RIGHT FOR YOU
TO KEEP THE HURTS AWAY.

IT DOES NOT MATTER WHAT YOUR AGE
YOU'LL ALWAYS BE MY BABY BOY.

WE WALK THROUGH MY DREAMS
AND TALK OF THINGS TO COME.
AND THEN THE DREAM GROWS DARK AND DIM
I FEEL YOUR HAND LEAVE MINE.
I FEEL YOUR WARM GENTLE KISS
AND WAKE TO THE TEARS ON MY CHEEK.
MY BABY BOY IS GONE.

Joan Molinaro

Eleanor Roosevelt wrote about the courage it takes to face our fears. She spoke from a personal sense of loss, during a time of global uncertainty.

PAINFULLY, STEP BY STEP, I LEARNED TO STARE DOWN EACH OF MY FEARS, CONQUER IT, ATTAIN THE HARD-EARNED COURAGE TO GO ON TO THE NEXT. ONLY THEN WAS I REALLY FREE.

OF ALL THE KNOWLEDGE THAT WE ACQUIRE IN LIFE THIS IS THE MOST DIFFICULT. BUT IT IS ALSO THE MOST REWARDING. WITH EACH VICTORY, NO MATTER HOW GREAT THE COST OR HOW AGONIZING AT THE TIME, THERE COMES INCREASED CONFIDENCE AND STRENGTH TO HELP MEET THE NEXT FEAR.

I HAVEN'T EVER BELIEVED THAT ANYTHING SUPPORTED BY FEAR CAN STAND AGAINST FREEDOM FROM FEAR.... COURAGE IS MORE EXHILARATING THAN FEAR AND IN THE LONG RUN IT IS EASIER. WE DO NOT HAVE TO BECOME HEROES OVERNIGHT. JUST A STEP AT A TIME, MEETING EACH THING THAT COMES UP, DISCOVERING WE HAVE THE STRENGTH TO STARE IT DOWN.

My father, Gregg Froehner, was a Port Authority police officer.
This is a poem that I would like to read to you today.

LIFE IS FOR ME AND IS SHINING!

. . .

I DO NOT WANT
FIRE SCREAMING UP TO THE SKY.
I DO NOT WANT
FAMILIES KILLED IN THEIR DOORWAYS.

LIFE IS FOR US, FOR THE CHILDREN.
LIFE IS FOR MOTHERS AND FATHERS,
LIFE IS FOR THE TALL GIRLS AND BOYS
IN THE HIGH SCHOOL ON HENDERSON STREET,
IS FOR THE PEOPLE IN AFRIKAN TENTS,
THE PEOPLE IN ENGLISH CATHEDRALS,
THE PEOPLE IN INDIAN COURTYARDS;
THE PEOPLE IN COTTAGES ALL OVER THE WORLD.

LIFE IS FOR US, AND IS SHINING.
WE HAVE A RIGHT TO SING.

Kathleen Froehner

Six decades ago, Winston Churchill's beloved country also suffered a terrible blow and faced what seemed to be insurmountable dangers and despair.

He taught me, and I remember on September 11, that he always believed, and we believe that people who live in freedom have something to live for, something to fight for, and even something to die for. And they will prevail over those who live in oppression. Winston Churchill taught us that our ideas and ideals of freedom and democracy will prevail.

He said:

WE SHALL NOT FAIL OR FALTER; WE SHALL NOT WEAKEN OR TIRE. NEITHER THE SUDDEN SHOCK OF BATTLE NOR THE LONG-DRAWN TRIALS OF VIGILANCE AND EXERTION WILL WEAR US DOWN.

He also said:

REPAIR THE WASTE. REBUILD THE RUINS. HEAL THE WOUNDS. CROWN THE VICTORS. COMFORT THE BROKEN AND BROKEN-HEARTED. THERE IS THE BATTLE WE HAVE WON TO FIGHT. THERE IS THE VICTORY WE HAVE NOW TO WIN. LET US GO FORWARD TOGETHER.

CLOSING

I want to thank the children of New York for helping us commemorate
this day. Their world is still in the making. As a mayor and a father, I hope it
will be a wise and just world. And that our city will always be the place where
people live in peace.

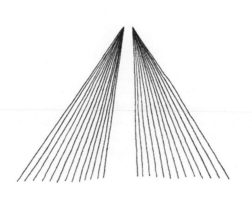

2004
**THE LOSS OF A CHILD**

INTRODUCTION

Today, again, we meet in great sadness. We come here to remember, and to ask the country and the world to remember, the names of those we lost three years ago. We will never forget that each person was someone's son or daughter. On behalf of all their parents, we have asked parents and grandparents who lost a child to lead our ceremonies.

At this time, please join us and all New Yorkers in a moment of silence.

.............................

It has been said that a child that loses a parent is an orphan. A man who loses his wife is a widower. A woman who loses her husband is a widow. There is no name for a parent who loses a child, for there is no word to describe this pain.

There is a room near this site – just a few yards away – called the Family Room. Families have been invited to come there, to be alone with their grief and their memories, to leave a picture or keepsake of their loved one, and write down what is in their hearts. Today, we've invited some of those parents and grandparents to share those feelings with us.

All the words you will hear will come either from them, or from what has been written over the ages, to give expression to their grief and comfort to their loss.

MY DAUGHTER WAS ON FLIGHT 11

My daughter, Sara Elizabeth Low, was a flight attendant on American Airlines Flight 11.

On October 28, 2001, my wife Bobbie and I came here for the first memorial service at Ground Zero. The Towers' ruins were still smoldering, and after that painful ceremony I scribbled these lines:

DREAMS BURN AWAY AS THE MORNING MIST; IN THE HEAT OF FATE'S RESOLVE.

We have left those lines in the back of a tribute booklet in the Family Room. We have been back to that room many times since. When I go into the room and look around at all the photos of the smiling faces of the young, beautiful, talented lives that were lost, their promises unfulfilled, their dreams burnt away, I think of a line from a 9/11 poem by an American Airlines pilot: "My God, what a wrenching loss!"

READING OF THE NAMES

Over two thousand years ago, when King David was told of the death of his son, he spoke the words that surely every parent today can understand.

THE KING WENT UP TO THE CHAMBER OVER THE GATE, AND WEPT; AND AS HE WENT, THUS HE SAID: 'O MY SON ABSALOM, MY SON, MY SON ABSALOM! WOULD I HAD DIED FOR THEE, O ABSALOM, MY SON, MY SON!'

We have asked the parents and grandparents to read the names of those who died.

A MOTHER SHARES A POEM

My son Nick worked on the 89th floor of Tower Two. We left this poem at the Family Center, because, Nicky, it describes how much we miss you.

REMEMBERING YOU IS EASY.
WE DO IT EVERY DAY.
IT'S THE HEARTACHE OF LOSING YOU,
THAT NEVER GOES AWAY.
WE THOUGHT OF YOU WITH LOVE TODAY,
BUT THAT IS NOTHING NEW,
WE THOUGHT ABOUT YOU YESTERDAY,
AND THE DAY BEFORE THAT TOO —
YOUR MEMORY IS OUR KEEPSAKE
WITH WHICH WE WILL NEVER PART.
GOD HAS YOU IN HIS KEEPING,
WE HAVE YOU IN OUR HEARTS.
OUR HEARTS STILL ACHE IN SADNESS
AND SECRET TEARS WILL FLOW —
WHAT IT MEANT TO LOSE YOU —
NO ONE WILL EVER KNOW!

All our love, Mom, Dad, Nicole, and Jay

Nancy Brandemarti

IF TEARS COULD BRING YOU BACK

Even after the victories of World War II, Dwight Eisenhower, who saw too many young sons die, wrote:

THERE'S NO TRAGEDY IN LIFE LIKE THE DEATH OF A CHILD; THINGS NEVER GET BACK TO THE WAY THEY WERE.

On the wall of the Family Room, a woman who lost her son put his picture on the wall and wrote this beside it:

TO THE WORLD HE MAY HAVE BEEN JUST ONE PERSON, BUT TO ME, HE WAS THE WORLD.

In one of the scrapbooks that sits on a table nearby, another mother wrote this poem and inscribed it to her daughter:

IF TEARS COULD BRING YOU BACK TO ME,
YOU'D BE HERE BY MY SIDE
FOR GOD COULD FILL A RIVER FULL
WITH ALL THE TEARS I'VE CRIED.
IF I COULD HAVE ONE WISH COME TRUE,
I'D ASK OF GOD IN PRAYER
TO LET ME HAVE JUST ONE MORE DAY
TO SHOW HOW MUCH I CARE.
IF LOVE COULD REACH TO HEAVEN'S SHORE,
I'D QUICKLY COME FOR YOU.
MY HEART WOULD BUILD A BRIDGE OF LOVE,
ONE WIDE ENOUGH FOR TWO.

To the parents and grandparents of our heroes, God bless you.
We will never forget.

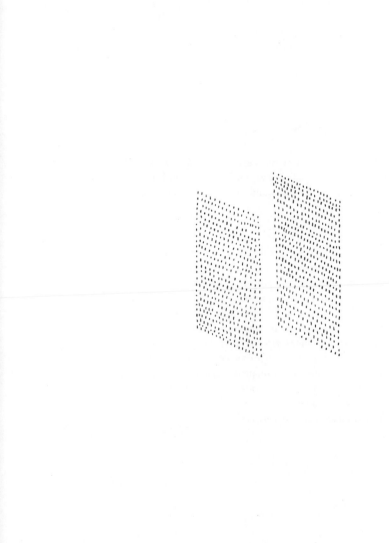

LETTER FROM ABRAHAM LINCOLN

In the fall of 1864, President Lincoln wrote a letter to a widow who had lost five sons in the Civil War. His words apply just as much today. In it, Lincoln poured out not just his own feelings, but the heart and soul of the country. The letter reads as follows:

DEAR MADAM:

I HAVE BEEN SHOWN IN THE FILES OF THE WAR DEPARTMENT A STATEMENT OF THE ADJUTANT GENERAL OF MASSACHUSETTS, THAT YOU ARE THE MOTHER OF FIVE SONS WHO HAVE DIED GLORIOUSLY ON THE FIELD OF BATTLE.

I FEEL HOW WEAK AND FRUITLESS MUST BE ANY WORDS OF MINE WHICH SHOULD ATTEMPT TO BEGUILE YOU FROM THE GRIEF OF A LOSS SO OVERWHELMING. BUT I CANNOT REFRAIN FROM TENDERING TO YOU THE CONSOLATION THAT MAY BE FOUND IN THE THANKS OF THE REPUBLIC THEY DIED TO SAVE.

I PRAY THAT OUR HEAVENLY FATHER MAY ASSUAGE THE ANGUISH OF YOUR BEREAVEMENT, AND LEAVE YOU ONLY THE CHERISHED MEMORY OF THE LOVED AND LOST, AND THE SOLEMN PRIDE THAT MUST BE YOURS, TO HAVE LAID SO COSTLY A SACRIFICE UPON THE ALTAR OF FREEDOM.

YOURS, VERY SINCERELY AND RESPECTFULLY,

ABRAHAM LINCOLN

A NOTE DISCOVERED

We found this note tucked into the corner of a scrapbook in the Family Center. Its paper was slightly torn, as though it had been held too tightly, as tightly as a mother holds her child's hand.

WHEN YOU REMEMBER ME,
IT MEANS THAT YOU HAVE CARRIED SOMETHING OF WHO I AM WITH YOU.
THAT I HAVE LEFT SOME MARK OF WHO I AM, ON WHO YOU ARE.
IT MEANS THAT EVEN AFTER I DIE, YOU CAN STILL SEE MY FACE,
AND HEAR MY VOICE,
AND SPEAK TO ME IN YOUR HEART.
FOR AS LONG AS YOU REMEMBER ME,
I AM NEVER ENTIRELY LOST.

MY SON AN UNKNOWN HERO

My son's name was Keithroy. He was a firefighter with the New York City Fire Department. My grandniece, Alison, and her classmates wrote this poem for him. It is called "An Unknown Hero."

TO MANY OF US HE WAS A FACE UNKNOWN.
A MAN WHOSE COURAGE WAS BRAVELY SHOWN.
YES, IT HAPPENED THAT DREADFUL DAY,
WHEN THE ENTIRE COUNTRY WEPT AND PRAYED.

TO SAVE OTHERS HE GAVE HIS LIFE.
LEAVING BEHIND A CHILD, KEITHROY.
WITHOUT A THOUGHT HE WENT INSIDE.
DO YOU THINK HE WAS TERRIFIED?

CHEERING HIM ON WAS GOD ABOVE,
GIVING HIM COURAGE AND GIVING HIM LOVE.

My Keith, we all love you and miss you.

**Pearl Maynard**

CLOSING

I want to thank the parents and grandparents for helping us commemorate this day. As a father, I know that their sadness can never be reckoned. Our hearts will be with them the rest of their days.

Our hope today, as it is every day, is that our city will be a place where all people can live in peace, so their dreams can reach skyward.

2005

**THE LOSS OF A SIBLING**

INTRODUCTION

Today, again, we are a city that meets in sadness. We come here to remember the names of those we lost four years ago. The greatest honor we can do them is to remember them not just as they were in death, but as they were in life. We have asked their sisters and brothers, those who grew up with them in childhood and knew them in the prime of their lives, to lead today's ceremonies.

At this time, please join us and all New Yorkers in a moment of silence.

....................................

The ties between brothers and sisters are special ones. Their lives are entwined from childhood, sharing a common bond of parents and the years of their youth.

Siblings know each other as no other person ever can, the one you depend on to walk with you, in times of trouble and in times of joy.

As we listen today to these sisters and brothers, we are reminded that there are ties between all men and women. That we are all linked to one another in our common humanity - that in a fundamental way, we are all brothers and sisters.

We have asked the siblings of those who died to help us remember the bright lives and legacies of those who perished in this place.

MY BROTHER LIVED IN TECHNICOLOR

My older brother John lived in technicolor. He taught me to wear bright colors and to love life. So I wore this bright pink shirt today to honor him and to fill the day with his great zest for living.

At home, we called John by his Greek name – Yanni. When he walked in the door, the whole house lit up. And I'm sure heaven lit up when he got there too. My brother wanted me to understand that each day should be lived to the fullest. That life is short and that I should to try to find happiness, even when I am surrounded by sadness. As we all are today.

When I think of John, I think about a man who had a gift for making those around him feel good about being alive. I hope I'll carry the lessons he taught me all through my life. I am proud that he graced this earth for 31 years and made such a lasting impression on so many people.

I am so proud to call him my brother.

Anthoula Katsimatides

READING OF THE NAMES

Today, as we recite the names of those we lost, our hearts turn as well toward London, our sister city, remembering those she has just lost as well.
And to Americans suffering in the aftermath of Hurricane Katrina, our deepest sympathies go out to you this day.

In difficult times as these, I think of the words of the great American poet Carl Sandburg:

TIME IS A GREAT TEACHER.
WHO CAN LIVE WITHOUT HOPE?

IN THE DARKNESS WITH A GREAT BUNDLE OF GRIEF THE PEOPLE MARCH.

On this fourth anniversary of 9/11, the one miracle we can perform is to go on living, to preserve, protect, and celebrate the value of life, and to remember those who died here not as strangers, but as our brothers and sisters.

Today, the sisters and brothers will read the names of those who died.

A BAND OF BROTHERS

I am here today to honor not one brother – my younger brother Tom – but a band of brothers.

Tom and I worked on the 105th floor – at different times with different brothers. Not just colleagues or coworkers – extraordinary men who became an extraordinary family. Brothers. Right here. Right on this spot. At the top of the world. A family who left their mark by how they lived their lives. From their first day to their last.

I am here today with a message they would deliver if only they could. Define us not by how we left – but by how we lived. By how we laughed. By how we loved. That's what they'd say. Make us the reason you embrace life – not the reason you don't. It's your spirit that keeps ours alive. That's what they'd say.

We hear you. Our hearts may be broken. Our spirit is not. That's what we need to say. True honor demands nothing less.

Thanks boys – I love ya'. I'll see ya' just a little further down the road. That's what I say.

Chris Burke

REMEMBER

I am so deeply moved to hear the individual stories of brothers and sisters, to learn about the lives of those who died here. For we all know that no matter how many fall, each life tells a unique story. Each death diminishes us all.

The poet Christina Rossetti wrote this about remembering those we have loved and lost:

REMEMBER ME WHEN I AM GONE AWAY,
   GONE FAR AWAY INTO THE SILENT LAND;
   WHEN YOU CAN NO MORE HOLD ME BY THE HAND,
NOR I HALF TURN TO GO YET TURNING STAY.
REMEMBER ME WHEN NO MORE DAY BY DAY
   YOU TELL ME OF OUR FUTURE THAT YOU PLANNED:
   ONLY REMEMBER ME; YOU UNDERSTAND
IT WILL BE LATE TO COUNSEL THEN OR PRAY.
YET IF YOU SHOULD FORGET ME FOR A WHILE
   AND AFTERWARDS REMEMBER, DO NOT GRIEVE:
   FOR IF THE DARKNESS AND CORRUPTION LEAVE
   A VESTIGE OF THE THOUGHTS THAT ONCE I HAD,
BETTER BY FAR YOU SHOULD FORGET AND SMILE
   THAN THAT YOU SHOULD REMEMBER AND BE SAD.

TO HIS DEAREST SISTER

Behind me, across the street, keeping watch over this site, is a place called the Family Room. Family members go there to leave a picture or a keepsake, and to write down what is in their hearts.

Every year that we return here on the anniversary of that terrible day we come to keep a promise: to remember those who died, not just as names or as part of a large number, but as individuals, whose lives still burn bright.

We found a poem in the Family Room, pinned to a photograph of a smiling young woman. It was left there by her brother, with a handwritten note across the top that read, "This is for you, my dearest sister." Today, I am sure, it speaks for what all the families feel in their hearts.

I'D LIKE THE MEMORY OF ME TO BE A HAPPY ONE.
I'D LIKE TO LEAVE AN AFTERGLOW OF SMILES WHEN LIFE IS DONE.
I'D LIKE TO LEAVE AN ECHO WHISPERING SOFTLY DOWN THE WAYS,
OF HAPPY TIMES AND LAUGHING TIMES AND BRIGHT AND SUNNY DAYS.
I'D LIKE THE TEARS OF THOSE WHO GRIEVE, TO DRY BEFORE THE SUN.
OF HAPPY MEMORIES THAT I LEAVE WHEN LIFE IS DONE.

YOU ARE ALWAYS IN THE HEART

How did New Yorkers respond to September 11 with such strength and compassion? The reason is that we're all Americans. People who have the blessings of freedom have more strength than they often realize, and they can call on that strength when they are put under attack. We help and support each other at our times of greatest trial. And that's what you all do.

Everyone who lost someone on September 11, 2001 – all of you here today who lost a sister or brother – should know that their loved one helped save the spirit of our nation on its day of greatest attack. They not only saved lives, they saved our country.

I have no brother or sister. You are now all my brothers and sisters. We all stand together to help each other and to help those who need our help in the future. We remember forever all the brothers and sisters that we lost on that day and they are all heroes.

Katherine Mansfield wrote movingly of the unbreakable bond shared by brothers and sisters:

BLESS YOU, MY DARLING, AND REMEMBER YOU ARE ALWAYS IN THE HEART — OH TUCKED SO CLOSE THERE IS NO CHANCE OF ESCAPE — OF YOUR SISTER.

MY BABY BROTHER

I am here to remember Gonj, my baby brother – a handsome, outgoing
young man who I adored from the day he was born. He loved helping people,
which is what made him love his job as a Port Authority police officer.
Then he convinced me to become a police officer – a job and a chance to help
people, which will always make me think of him.

There are some song lyrics which help me express what I want to say to
him today:

LETTING GO CAN BE THE HARDEST THING TO DO.
WHEN YOU TRULY CARE ABOUT SOMEONE
YOU CAN'T SAY GOODBYE ENOUGH TIMES TO MAKE ALL THE FEELINGS LAST A LIFETIME.
BUT ALL THE MEMORIES NEVER GO AWAY.

Gonj, please know that Mom and our two younger sisters, Elfia and Anane,
hold on every day to every memory we have of you. We miss you. We love you
and always will.

Kyra Houston

BEGIN WITH HOW THEY LIVED

All along the walls of the Family Room are photographs brimming with life: people in their summer T-shirts and in their wedding gowns. People holding their children and laughing with their friends.

As the days and years pass, let our remembrance of them be what keeps reminding us of the value of every human life. One brother left this note pinned to a photograph:

MY BROTHER TJ WAS TAKEN FROM US. WHILE WE ARE ALL DEEPLY SADDENED BY THE EVENTS THAT LED TO HIS DEATH, WE NEED TO REMEMBER TJ NOT BY HOW HE DIED BUT BY HOW HE LIVED. TO BE A GREAT MAN, YOU FIRST MUST BE A GOOD MAN. MY BROTHER WAS A GOOD MAN. WHEN WE REMEMBER HIM, LET US ALWAYS BEGIN WITH THAT.

CLOSING

I want to thank the brothers and sisters for helping us commemorate this
day. We know their bonds of affection will never be lost or broken. Today, as
every day, it is our hope that we join together as a city, to affirm life even in
the midst of sadness.

In the words of the great American poet Wallace Stevens:

AFTER THE FINAL NO THERE COMES A YES
AND ON THAT YES THE FUTURE WORLD DEPENDS.

INTRODUCTION

Five years have come and five years have gone – and still we stand together
as one. We come back to this place to remember the heartbreaking anniversary
and each person who died here. Those known and unknown to us, whose
absence is always with us. This year, we have asked their spouses, partners,
and significant others to lead these ceremonies, not in the first flush of despair,
but with the saving grace of memory.

At this time, please join us and all New Yorkers in a moment of silence.

...............................

It surely cannot be easy to come to this site and speak out loud the name of
the person you had thought would always be next to you, the one with whom you
had hoped to face the world.

We stand by your side, yet who can know what is in your hearts.

TO MY HUSBAND

My husband, Robert, worked at Cantor Fitzgerald. We had been married
only for nine years, though it felt as if we had shared a lifetime together because
of all that we had been through.

The light of his life were our three children, Ryan and our twins, Kyle
and Nicole.

Of all the many things I wish I could still tell him, there is one thing my heart
wants to say above all the rest. Feelings best expressed in the words of an
American song:

HOW MUCH DO I LOVE YOU?
I'LL TELL YOU NO LIE:
HOW DEEP IS THE OCEAN,
HOW HIGH IS THE SKY?
HOW MANY TIMES A DAY
DO I THINK OF YOU?
HOW MANY ROSES
ARE SPRINKLED WITH DEW?
HOW FAR WOULD I TRAVEL
TO BE WHERE YOU ARE?
HOW FAR IS THE JOURNEY
FROM HERE TO A STAR?
AND IF I EVER LOST YOU,
HOW MUCH WOULD I CRY?
HOW DEEP IS THE OCEAN,
HOW HIGH IS THE SKY?

Susan Sliwak

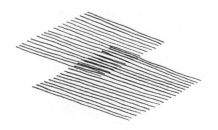

This year the names of all who died will be read by the men and women with whom they shared their lives and themselves.

Today, as they help us remember those we lost, the words of the New York poet Mark Van Doren remind us:

NOTHING IS DEAD OR DIFFERENT —
TELL HIM, AND MAKE SURE.
FOR HE MUST UNDERSTAND THAT I
AND NOT MY WOUNDS ENDURE.

MY WIFE RAN INTO THE TOWER

I am the husband of New York City Police Officer Moira Smith, who five years ago ran into the South Tower because she believed that a life lived in service of others was the only one worth living. She never hesitated when there was work to be done. And that is how she would want our seven-year-old daughter, Patricia, to remember her.

I've been thinking about what Moira would be doing today if she were here with us. She'd be concerned for her fellow officers, their health and safety. She'd be protecting the people of the city she loved, defending the country she loved. Keeping it from harm. She would be raising the child she loved more than anything on earth.

But more importantly, Moira would be about the business of living. She would be making us smile when we want to frown and laugh when we want to cry. Police Officer Moira Smith did not survive that day, and the world is a less safe, less fun, and less caring place because of it.

I am honored to have been her husband. I am grateful to have our child to raise, and to help her understand that her mother was – and still is – the pride of New York City.

DIRGE WITHOUT MUSIC (excerpt)

Of all those we know in life, it is our chosen mate – the companion of our days – to whom we entrust our deepest selves. And in turn, we celebrate that person for exactly who they are. In their passing, an essential piece of us is torn away.

The poet Edna St. Vincent Millay wrote:

THE ANSWERS QUICK AND KEEN, THE HONEST LOOK, THE LAUGHTER, THE LOVE, – THEY ARE GONE.
...I KNOW. BUT I DO NOT APPROVE.
MORE PRECIOUS WAS THE LIGHT IN YOUR EYES THAN ALL THE ROSES IN THE WORLD.

. . .

GENTLY THEY GO, THE BEAUTIFUL, THE TENDER, THE KIND;
QUIETLY THEY GO, THE INTELLIGENT, THE WITTY, THE BRAVE.
I KNOW. BUT I DO NOT APPROVE. AND I AM NOT RESIGNED.

WHAT IS SUCCESS

Five years from the date of the attack that changed our world, we've come back to remember the valor of those we lost; those who innocently went to work that day and the brave souls who went in after them. We also have come to be ever mindful of the courage of those who grieve for them, and the light that still lives in their hearts.

As we honor those who died, we ask, what is a successful life? One hundred years ago, an essay tried to answer that question and has endured to become an American classic:

TO LAUGH OFTEN AND LOVE MUCH; TO GAIN THE RESPECT OF INTELLIGENT PEOPLE AND WIN THE LOVE OF LITTLE CHILDREN; TO EARN THE APPRECIATION OF HONEST CRITICS — TO APPRECIATE BEAUTY, TO FIND THE BEST IN OTHERS — TO LEAVE THE WORLD BETTER THAN YOU FOUND IT — WHETHER BY A HEALTHY CHILD, A GARDEN PATCH OR REDEEMED SOCIAL CONDITIONS — TO KNOW EVEN ONE LIFE HAS BREATHED EASIER BECAUSE YOU LIVED — THIS IS TO HAVE SUCCEEDED.

God bless all of those that we lost. God bless all of you who mourn for them and live on in their spirit.

TURN AGAIN TO LIFE

With heavy heart and much love, we have come to this sacred place to remember and honor together those we loved and lost. To all those who seek help to remember, we recall the words of the poet Mary Lee Hall, who sought to find in loss the comfort to go on:

IF I SHOULD DIE AND LEAVE YOU HERE A WHILE,
BE NOT LIKE OTHERS SORE UNDONE,
WHO KEEP LONG VIGIL BY THE SILENT DUST.
FOR MY SAKE TURN AGAIN TO LIFE AND SMILE,
NERVING THY HEART AND TREMBLING HAND
TO DO SOMETHING TO COMFORT OTHER HEARTS THAN THINE.
COMPLETE THESE DEAR UNFINISHED TASKS OF MINE
AND I PERCHANCE MAY THEREIN COMFORT YOU.

God bless you all from the bottom of my heart and from all of us who love you.

SHE MADE ME LAUGH

My partner, Patricia McAneney, worked in Tower One of the World Trade Center. I am here today to remember and to honor her.

Pat was a kind and caring woman born with a twinkle in her eye, the gift of laughter and the ability to share it with others. She taught me that I could laugh at myself.

A die-hard Mets fan, she cheered in the spring and cried in the fall.

It was Pat's natural warmth that made people around her feel comfortable. But it was her dry sense of humor that kept you laughing and coming back for more.

There is a poem that says:

SO BITTER PAIN THAT NONE SHALL EVER FIND.
WHAT PLAGUE IS GREATER THAN THE GRIEF OF MIND.

No day has been the same without you – but the memories of your smile and laughter will hold me and all who loved you for years to come.

Margaret Cruz

CLOSING

I want to thank everyone for helping us commemorate this day: for giving a human face to the names engraved on our city's heart, and to the cherished dreams that will be left forever unfulfilled.

Even as we mourn their loss, we are ever mindful of what was written centuries ago:

YOUR CAUSE OF SORROW
MUST NOT BE MEASURED BY HIS WORTH, FOR THEN
IT HATH NO END.

For all Americans, this date will be forever entwined with sadness, but the memory of those we lost can burn with a softening brightness.

2007
**FIRST RESPONDERS**

INTRODUCTION

Today marks the sixth anniversary of the day that tore across our history
and our hearts.

We come together, again, as New Yorkers and as Americans, to share a loss
that cannot be measured, and to remember the names of those who
cannot be replaced.

This year, we have asked those who responded to the tragedy to help us lead
the ceremonies. Both the men and women in official uniform and the volunteers
who said, "These are my neighbors. Let me help."

At this time, please join us and all New Yorkers in a moment of silence.

. . . . . . . . . . . . . . . . . . . . . . . . . . . .

On that day, we felt isolated, but not for long and not from each other.
New Yorkers rushed to this site, not knowing which place was safe or if there
was more danger ahead. They weren't sure of anything, except that they
had to be here. Six years have passed, and our place is still by your side.

As the poet William Blake wrote centuries ago:

CAN I SEE ANOTHERS WOE,
AND NOT BE IN SORROW TOO.

Mayor Bloomberg

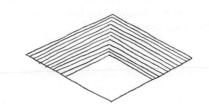

I IMAGINE HER AT OUR SIDE

My wife, Sol, worked in the South Tower.

Sol, since the first time I looked at you I knew you were the woman who would change my life. You became my wife and the mother of our children, Alexis and Shayla. You gave me what I could not find anywhere else – "True Love."

On my 40th birthday, you gave me a plaque which read: I always searched for someone who could make my dreams come true but I finally stopped my searching on the day that I found you.

Well, honey, those words mean more to me now than they meant back then. But more important than what I feel are the words that come from our daughters. This is what they wrote to you:

I IMAGINE YOU ALWAYS AT OUR SIDE, EVEN THOUGH YOU ARE FAR FROM US. TIME PASSES, BUT THE MEMORIES OF YOU, FULL OF LOVE, WILL BE OUR BEST GUIDE. WE LOVE YOU MOMMY.

Sol, our family will never feel complete again until God reunites us in heaven.

I would now like to thank my family, Mayor Bloomberg, Commissioner John Doherty, Borough Commissioner Phil Marino, and my extended family, the New York City Department of Sanitation, for all the support they have given me and my daughters over the past few years.

READING OF THE NAMES

In years past, the names of those we lost have been read by mothers and fathers, sons and daughters, sisters and brothers, spouses and significant others. Today, they are being read by those who stepped forward, who offered their arms into which those who grieved could fall.

Acts of kindness and bravery were given without a second thought. As a poet wrote over a century ago:

WE CANNOT LIVE FOR OURSELVES ALONE. A THOUSAND THREADS CONNECT YOU WITH YOUR FELLOW-MEN.

HE WAS THE QUIET ONE

My brother, Charles Gregory John, was a very caring, understanding, and loving son, brother, and father. He worked in the North Tower on the 82nd floor and was abruptly taken away from us in the prime of his life. Although he was my older brother, I miss him turning to me for advice and guidance.

Greg, we miss you at our family gathering and annual barbecue. The sight of you at the grill, making those perfect chicken and ribs. How delicious you made them taste. We laugh and wish you were still here with us.

In our family of six siblings, Gregory was the quiet one. The one with the playful spirit who brought out the smiles in each of us. While we have learned to smile again, we never do it without thinking of you. Every day, every month, and every year. We love and miss you Charles Gregory John.

·

NO MAN IS AN ISLAND

We stand today on this terrible threshold, remembering all that happened. We feel today, as we felt then, that we belong to one another, not because we are inhabitants of the same city or same country, but because we are all part of the same human story. Part of one community of our fellow human beings.

John Donne wrote these immortal words centuries ago:

NO MAN IS AN ISLAND, ENTIRE OF ITSELF; EVERY MAN IS A PIECE OF THE CONTINENT, A PART OF THE MAIN... ANY MAN'S DEATH DIMINISHES ME, BECAUSE I AM INVOLVED IN MANKIND; AND THEREFORE NEVER SEND TO KNOW FOR WHOM THE BELL TOLLS; IT TOLLS FOR THEE.

Governor Spitzer

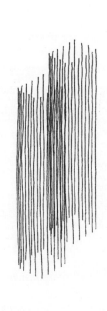

WHAT WE CAN GIVE

On this day six years ago and on the days that followed, in the midst of our great grief and turmoil, we witnessed uncompromising strength and resilience as a people. It was a day with no answers, but with an unending line of those who came forward to try to help one another.

Elie Wiesel wrote this about the blackest night a human being can know:

I HAVE LEARNED TWO LESSONS IN MY LIFE: FIRST, THERE ARE NO SUFFICIENT LITERARY, PSYCHOLOGICAL, OR HISTORICAL ANSWERS TO HUMAN TRAGEDY, ONLY MORAL ONES.

SECOND, JUST AS DESPAIR CAN COME TO ONE ANOTHER ONLY FROM OTHER HUMAN BEINGS, HOPE, TOO, CAN BE GIVEN TO ONE ONLY BY OTHER HUMAN BEINGS.

Mayor Giuliani

HER SON AND DAUGHTER

Nicholas:
Our mother, Catherine Chirls, passed away in the North Tower. She worked for Cantor Fitzgerald. She was my whole life, as she was for my sister and brother, who are here with me today. We miss her and love her more than ever. My sister, Sydney, would like to share a poem that our mother shared with us a few weeks before she passed away.

Sydney:
AUTUMN TO WINTER, WINTER INTO SPRING.
SPRING INTO SUMMER, SUMMER INTO FALL.
SO ROLLS THE CHANGING YEAR, AND SO WE CHANGE.
MOTION SO SWIFT, WE KNOW NOT THAT WE MOVE.

Thank you. We love you Mom.

IF WE CEASE TO HOLD EACH OTHER

A student remembered that day: "The expressions on everyone's faces told the whole story. No one knew what to say. Nobody knew what to do. Nobody had ever experienced anything like this before. The only truth was that everybody wanted to find a way to help."

We must never lose that feeling of connectedness. A necessity once described like this, by the great American novelist James Baldwin:

...THE EARTH IS ALWAYS SHIFTING, THE LIGHT IS ALWAYS CHANGING.... GENERATIONS DO NOT CEASE TO BE BORN, AND WE ARE RESPONSIBLE TO THEM BECAUSE WE ARE THE ONLY WITNESSES THEY HAVE. THE SEA RISES, THE LIGHT FAILS, LOVERS CLING TO EACH OTHER, AND CHILDREN CLING TO US. THE MOMENT WE CEASE TO HOLD EACH OTHER, THE MOMENT WE BREAK FAITH WITH ONE ANOTHER, THE SEA ENGULFS US AND THE LIGHT GOES OUT.

KATRINA'S SUN-DIAL (excerpt)

We have come today to lean on one another, to offer our solace and comfort. We join with you as you think of those you have lost, and remember them with joy and love.

The American poet Henry Van Dyke put into words the feelings we know all too well.

TIME IS
TOO SLOW FOR THOSE WHO WAIT,
TOO SWIFT FOR THOSE WHO FEAR,
TOO LONG FOR THOSE WHO GRIEVE,
TOO SHORT FOR THOSE WHO REJOICE;
BUT FOR THOSE WHO LOVE,
TIME IS NOT.

CLOSING

I want to thank the families and the responders for helping us today, by giving words to our memories and voice to the names that must never be forgotten.

On this anniversary day, we are guided by these words:

SADNESS FLIES ON THE WINGS OF THE MORNING AND OUT OF THE HEART OF DARKNESS COMES THE LIGHT.

And today, to that light, we entrust our grief and our gratitude, our disbelief and our hopes, and our dedication to the sanctity of this site and to the care of one another.

2008

**THE INTERNATIONAL FAMILY**

INTRODUCTION

Today marks the seventh anniversary of the day our world was broken. It lives forever in our hearts and our history, a tragedy that unites us in a common memory and a common story.

We return today as New Yorkers, Americans, and global citizens, remembering that innocent people from over 90 nations and territories lost their lives together that day. At this ceremony, we will turn to the poets and writers from around the world, who give expression to the universality of our feelings, to the emotions that unite us, and remind us how alike we all really are.

At this time, please join us and all New Yorkers in a moment of silence.

....................................

We come each year to stand alongside those who loved and lost the most, to bear witness to the day which began like any other, and ended as none ever has.

On that day, lives – very precious to this earth – were cut short, and the entire world was made less for it. As the Irish proverb reminds us:

DEATH LEAVES A HEARTACHE NO ONE CAN HEAL,
LOVE LEAVES A MEMORY NO ONE CAN STEAL.

THREE YOUNG CHILDREN

Alexander:
Our father, John Salamone, worked for Cantor Fitzgerald in the North Tower. Today my brother and I are wearing his soccer shirts.

I remember playing in the yard with him, I remember him pulling me in my wagon. He was strong, he always made me feel safe. He was funny, he always made me laugh. I wish I could remember more, but we were so young when he died. But I do remember how much he loved us and I know how much we miss him.

Aidan:
But even though he is gone, he is still with us and helps us to be better people. For our dad, we try to be kinder and help people in need. We work a little harder in school, we try our best in our sports. For our dad, we hope to make a difference one day in the world, he would be so proud of that. My dad died on 9/11 but he is not gone. Just look at each of our faces and you will see him shine through every day.

Anna:
We love you Daddy.

READING OF THE NAMES

This morning we stand again as one family, one community of the world.
As in past years, the names of those who died will be read by their families.
Joining them are the young faces of our future, students from around the
world, attending our city's universities, who come on behalf of each country
that lost someone that day.

They help us remember that now, as then, the feelings of grief, sorrow, loss,
and consolation are ones we all share.

As the proverb of the Sioux Indians reminds us:

WITH ALL BEINGS AND ALL THINGS WE SHALL BE AS RELATIVES.

The great French writer Albert Camus wrote about the feelings we have when we have lost a loved one:

LOSING A LOVED ONE, UNCERTAINTY ABOUT WHAT WE ARE, THESE ARE DEPRIVATIONS THAT GIVE RISE TO OUR WORST SUFFERING.

SO MANY THINGS ARE SUSCEPTIBLE OF BEING LOVED THAT SURELY NO DISCOURAGEMENT CAN BE FINAL. TO KNOW HOW TO SUFFER, TO KNOW HOW TO LOVE, AND, WHEN EVERYTHING COLLAPSES, TO TAKE EVERYTHING UP ONCE MORE, SIMPLY, THE RICHER FROM SUFFERING, ALMOST HAPPY FROM THE AWARENESS OF OUR MISERY.

MY BROTHER OPENED OUR EYES

My awesome little brother, Craig William Staub, worked on the 89th floor of Tower Two.

How do I best describe a man who brought a love of life and a wacky sense of humor into every room he entered, whose purity of heart was obvious, even to strangers. Maybe that's why a couple he met on vacation asked him to be best man at their wedding.

In his brief life, Craig managed to achieve great success without ever putting on airs. And he went out of his way when someone needed help – he even collected leftovers at company events to hand out to the homeless.

As many times as I have tried to make sense of his loss, and tried to understand how this could all be part of God's plan, finally something has occurred to me. Craig left us way too early, but in doing so he bestowed upon us a great gift – the gift of inspiration. His loss helped open our eyes – not just to see and appreciate him more clearly, but to endeavor, more than ever, to live our lives by following his example. To love life and help one another.

Craig, on behalf of everyone in our family, thank you for being our inspiration. We will always love you.

Carolyn Staub Bilelis

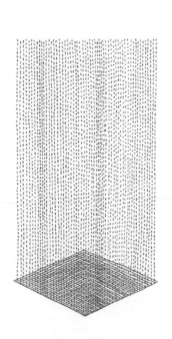

TRY TO PRAISE THE MUTILATED WORLD (excerpt)

No matter what country we come from or what language we speak, everyone remembers the same day, shares the same feelings, sheds the same tears, and goes on living in the same world.

On this September morning, we should keep in our hearts the words of the Polish poet Adam Zagajewski, who wrote:

TRY TO PRAISE THE MUTILATED WORLD.
REMEMBER JUNE'S LONG DAYS,
AND WILD STRAWBERRIES, DROPS OF ROSÉ WINE....
REMEMBER THE MOMENTS WHEN WE WERE TOGETHER
IN A WHITE ROOM AND THE CURTAIN FLUTTERED.
RETURN IN THOUGHT TO THE CONCERT WHERE MUSIC FLARED.
YOU GATHERED ACORNS IN THE PARK IN AUTUMN
AND LEAVES EDDIED OVER THE EARTH'S SCARS.
PRAISE THE MUTILATED WORLD
AND THE GRAY FEATHER A THRUSH LOST,
AND THE GENTLE LIGHT THAT STRAYS AND VANISHES
AND RETURNS.

MY FATHER WAS A PASTRY CHEF

My father, Norberto, was a pastry chef at Windows on the World in Tower One. For ten years, he made many fancy and famous desserts, but the sweetest dessert he made was the marble cake he made for us at home. From the time I was a little girl, I remember him baking in our kitchen, and how my sisters, Tatiana and Jacquelin, and my mom would sit around the kitchen table eating his cake and talking about our lives.

It's been seven years since we've all been able to sit around the table. So many things have happened in my life that I would have wanted to tell my Poppi while I ate the marble cake he made with all his love. I joined the New York City Police Department. I got married, and my husband and I moved to a beautiful new house and had a baby, Kyle Norberto. And now, I'm also going to college. I know he would have been proud of me, and been a wonderful grandfather.

Whenever we parted, Poppi would say, "Te amo. Vaya con Dios." And this morning, I want to say the same thing to you, Poppi. I love you. Go with God.

Catherine Hernandez

FOR THE FALLEN (excerpt)

In his poem "For The Fallen" the English poet Laurence Binyon wrote:

THEY SHALL GROW NOT OLD, AS WE THAT ARE LEFT GROW OLD:
AGE SHALL NOT WEARY THEM, NOR THE YEARS CONDEMN.
AT THE GOING DOWN OF THE SUN AND IN THE MORNING
WE WILL REMEMBER THEM.

For seven years, we have come back here to be together, to feel how the entire world is linked in our circle of sorrow, and to remember that those we loved are never truly lost. The poem reminds us how brightly their memories burn.

BUT WHERE OUR DESIRES ARE AND OUR HOPES PROFOUND,
FELT AS A WELL-SPRING THAT IS HIDDEN FROM SIGHT,
TO THE INNERMOST HEART OF THEIR OWN LAND THEY ARE KNOWN
AS THE STARS ARE KNOWN TO THE NIGHT;

AS THE STARS THAT SHALL BE BRIGHT WHEN WE ARE DUST,
MOVING IN MARCHES UPON THE HEAVENLY PLAIN,
AS THE STARS ARE STARRY IN THE TIME OF OUR DARKNESS,
TO THE END, TO THE END, THEY REMAIN.

Mayor Giuliani

DROP BY DROP UPON THE HEART

At another moment of national grief – the death of Martin Luther King, Jr. – Robert Kennedy spoke these words of solace, written by the ancient Greek poet Aeschylus:

HE WHO LEARNS MUST SUFFER.

AND EVEN IN OUR SLEEP, PAIN THAT CANNOT FORGET

FALLS DROP BY DROP UPON THE HEART,

AND IN OUR OWN DESPAIR, AGAINST OUR WILL,

COMES WISDOM BY THE AWFUL GRACE OF GOD.

**Governor Pataki**

THE GUEST HOUSE

Although our hearts will never get used to losing those we loved, we know that there is joy to be found in remembering them.

And in every corner of the world, for as long as men and women have lived, there will be the gift of love and the bittersweet moments to remember its loss. The 13th-century Persian poet Rumi understood this. In his poem "The Guest House" he wrote:

THIS BEING HUMAN IS A GUEST HOUSE.
EVERY MORNING A NEW ARRIVAL.

A JOY, A DEPRESSION, A MEANNESS,
SOME MOMENTARY AWARENESS COMES
AS AN UNEXPECTED VISITOR.

WELCOME AND ENTERTAIN THEM ALL!
EVEN IF THEY'RE A CROWD OF SORROWS,
WHO VIOLENTLY SWEEP YOUR HOUSE
EMPTY OF ITS FURNITURE,
STILL, TREAT EACH GUEST HONORABLY.
HE MAY BE CLEARING YOU OUT
FOR SOME NEW DELIGHT.

THE DARK THOUGHT, THE SHAME, THE MALICE,
MEET THEM AT THE DOOR LAUGHING,
AND INVITE THEM IN.

BE GRATEFUL FOR WHOEVER COMES,
BECAUSE EACH HAS BEEN SENT
AS A GUIDE FROM BEYOND.

CLOSING

The Polish poet Wislawa Szymborska wrote:

THIS TERRIFYING WORLD IS NOT DEVOID OF CHARMS,
OF THE MORNINGS
THAT MAKE WAKING UP WORTHWHILE.

And on this morning, I want to thank all the families and students for helping us today, and for giving us a picture of the possibility of the united human family.

Throughout our ceremony, poets from around the world have given voice to our feelings. It is fitting to end by returning home, to the words of the American poet Wendell Berry. May his grace note of hope help lift up this day and turn our wounded hearts toward tomorrow.

WHEN DESPAIR FOR THE WORLD GROWS IN ME
AND I WAKE IN THE NIGHT AT THE LEAST SOUND
IN FEAR OF WHAT MY LIFE AND MY CHILDREN'S LIVES MAY BE,
I GO AND LIE DOWN WHERE THE WOOD DRAKE
RESTS IN HIS BEAUTY ON THE WATER, AND THE GREAT HERON FEEDS.
I COME INTO THE PEACE OF WILD THINGS
WHO DO NOT TAX THEIR LIVES WITH FORETHOUGHT
OF GRIEF. I COME INTO THE PRESENCE OF STILL WATER.
AND I FEEL ABOVE ME THE DAY-BLIND STARS
WAITING WITH THEIR LIGHT. FOR A TIME
I REST IN THE GRACE OF THE WORLD, AND AM FREE.

2009
**A DAY OF SERVICE**

INTRODUCTION

Eight years we have come together to commemorate the anniversary
of this day.

Just as our hearts return to those we lost, we also remember all those who
spontaneously rushed forward to help – however and whomever they could.
Their compassionate and selfless acts are etched into our city's story.

Inspired by what they did that day, President Obama has designated 9/11 as
an "annually recognized National Day of Service and Remembrance." And,
appropriately, the City of New York has been the first to take up that call.

From this day forward, we will safeguard the memories of those who died
by rekindling the spirit of service that lit our city with hope and helped
to keep us strong.

At this time, please join us and all New Yorkers in a moment of silence.

..............................

Eight years ago, countless people played a part in history by doing something
to help another person, probably someone they didn't even know.
No one stopped to ask, if I can only do a little, should I bother doing anything
at all? Each act was a link in a continuous chain, that stopped us from falling
into cynicism and despair.

Reflecting on all she had seen in her life and in the halls of justice, the recently
retired Supreme Court Justice Sandra Day O'Connor said this:

WE DON'T ACCOMPLISH ANYTHING IN THIS WORLD ALONE...AND WHATEVER HAPPENS
IS THE RESULT OF THE WHOLE TAPESTRY OF ONE'S LIFE AND ALL THE WEAVINGS OF
INDIVIDUAL THREADS FROM ONE TO ANOTHER THAT CREATES SOMETHING.

**Mayor Bloomberg**

BECAUSE HE RAN TO HELP OTHERS

My brother Glenn was a partner at the law firm Holland & Knight, located just a few blocks from where we are standing. He was also a longtime volunteer firefighter and an EMT in our hometown of Jericho.

When the towers were hit, Glenn's instinct was to race from his place of safety toward the South Tower, toward the inferno and the people in danger.
He died when the South Tower collapsed.

My little brother is my greatest hero. Not just for the way he died, but for the way he lived. With acts large and small, Glenn always tried to help people - usually people he didn't even know. And like all firefighters, EMTs, and cops, he ran toward those in peril, to still their fears, and protect them from harm.

Glenn died as he lived. With purpose to his life, with a joy in connecting to people and the world he lived in.

What he did here inspired many of us to create a living legacy in honor of those who perished, an organization we call MyGoodDeed, which encourages people to help others in need, each 9/11. We are honored to play a part in making today a National Day of Service and Remembrance.

One of the ancient Greeks wrote:

WHAT YOU LEAVE BEHIND IS NOT WHAT IS ENGRAVED IN STONE MONUMENTS, BUT WHAT IS WOVEN INTO THE LIVES OF OTHERS.

Glenn, we know that the bright light of your life is woven not only into our memories, but into the lives of countless others, illuminating the world with hope, one person, one good deed at a time.

**Jay Winuk**

READING OF THE NAMES

It is the sacred duty of the living to carry within us the memories of those we lost. And while there is pain in remembering the loss, there is sweetness in remembering their lives.

As in years past, the names of those who died will be read by their families. This year, they will be joined by those who voluntarily give their time to help others throughout the year and throughout the city. They are truly the inheritors of the spirit shown here eight years ago.

WILD GEESE (excerpt)

There is one thing all Americans know to be true and which we remember most when we come to this site: in our joys and in our sorrows, we belong to one another. The poet Mary Oliver wrote:

TELL ME ABOUT DESPAIR, YOURS, AND I WILL TELL YOU MINE.
MEANWHILE THE WORLD GOES ON.
MEANWHILE THE SUN AND THE CLEAR PEBBLES OF THE RAIN
ARE MOVING ACROSS THE LANDSCAPES,
OVER THE PRAIRIES AND THE DEEP TREES,
THE MOUNTAINS AND THE RIVERS.
MEANWHILE THE WILD GEESE, HIGH IN THE CLEAN BLUE AIR,
ARE HEADING HOME AGAIN.
WHOEVER YOU ARE, NO MATTER HOW LONELY,
THE WORLD OFFERS ITSELF TO YOUR IMAGINATION,
CALLS TO YOU LIKE THE WILD GEESE, HARSH AND EXCITING —
OVER AND OVER ANNOUNCING YOUR PLACE
IN THE FAMILY OF THINGS.

GIFTS MY HUSBAND LEFT US

My husband, Cesar Amoranto Alviar, worked on the 94th floor of Tower One as an accountant.

How proud we were of him. We came from the Philippines in 1983 with our children, Christopher, Ginny, and Gemma. Eight years have passed, but sometimes it feels like everything just happened yesterday. The pain can be so sharp. Other times, I realize how much my life has changed.

My children have grown, my grandchildren – Riley, James, and Grayson – were born. Life has brought many gifts to us, his three brothers, two sisters, and their families. I wish he could be here to share them. But he can still be with us in the way we live our lives.

He taught us to be humble and patient with one another, to never hold on to anger or hate. In his words, "to find the strength to be gentle, and the courage to be kind." This is a poem that expresses how I feel:

i carry your heart with me(i carry it in
my heart)i am never without it(anywhere
i go you go,my dear;and whatever is done
by only me is your doing,my darling)
                              i fear
no fate(for you are my fate, my sweet)i want
no world(for beautiful you are my world,my true)
and it's you are whatever a moon has always meant
and whatever a sun will always sing is you

Cesar, we miss you. Thank you for sharing your life with me.

I DREAM'D IN A DREAM

One of this city's greatest sons, Walt Whitman, the poet with the heart full of all humanity, described how he saw New York:

I DREAM'D IN A DREAM I SAW A CITY INVINCIBLE TO THE ATTACKS
    OF THE WHOLE OF THE REST OF THE EARTH,
I DREAM'D THAT WAS THE NEW CITY OF FRIENDS,
NOTHING WAS GREATER THERE THAN THE QUALITY OF ROBUST LOVE, IT LED THE REST,
IT WAS SEEN EVERY HOUR IN THE ACTIONS OF THE MEN OF THAT CITY,
AND IN ALL THEIR LOOKS AND WORDS.

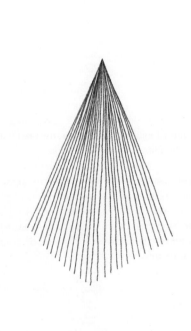

IF I CAN STOP ONE HEART FROM BREAKING

The great poet from Massachusetts, Emily Dickinson, spoke plainly
and profoundly:

IF I CAN STOP ONE HEART FROM BREAKING
I SHALL NOT LIVE IN VAIN
IF I CAN EASE ONE LIFE THE ACHING
OR COOL ONE PAIN

OR HELP ONE FAINTING ROBIN
UNTO HIS NEST AGAIN
I SHALL NOT LIVE IN VAIN.

Governor Corzine

HIS WAS A HELPING HAND

I am the brother-in-law of Firefighter Thomas J. Foley, who perished in the South Tower.

Tommy's life was always about giving and doing for others, from volunteering to the local fire department, to playing Santa for the kids at Christmas. All who knew and worked with him were inspired by his zest for life, his bright smile, and quick wit.

Tommy's true passion was to become a New York City firefighter. In July 1994, that dream came true. In his short career, he made many headline rescues, both with Squad 41 and with Rescue 3. Whenever he was questioned about his heroism, he always gave credit to everyone on the team who was involved.

We would like to ask you never to forget his sacrifice, and all those who lost their lives on September 11. May this day be remembered and revered by future generations, as a lesson in sorrow but also in humanity.

Tommy left behind his parents, Tom and Pat Foley, his sister, Joanne, and his brother, Danny, also a New York City firefighter with Rescue 3, and many nieces and nephews. We would like you to join us in honoring Tommy and all the others who perished by participating in the many events, scholarships, and foundations set up in their honor.

I know that Tommy would thank all the members of the FDNY for their courage and commitment, as well as others who worked tirelessly in the rescue and recovery efforts.

On behalf of Tommy and the Foley family, we'd also like to thank the brave men and women of our armed forces, both past and present, for their continued sacrifice and heroism.

Tommy we love and miss you. God bless America.

EVERYBODY CAN BE GREAT

## Martin Luther King, Jr. once said:

EVERYBODY CAN BE GREAT. BECAUSE ANYBODY CAN SERVE. YOU DON'T HAVE TO
HAVE A COLLEGE DEGREE TO SERVE. YOU DON'T HAVE TO MAKE YOUR SUBJECT AND
VERB AGREE TO SERVE....YOU ONLY NEED A HEART FULL OF GRACE. A SOUL
GENERATED BY LOVE.

## He also said,

EVERY MAN MUST DECIDE WHETHER HE WILL WALK IN THE LIGHT OF CREATIVE
ALTRUISM OR THE DARKNESS OF DESTRUCTIVE SELFISHNESS. THIS IS THE JUDGMENT.
LIFE'S MOST PERSISTENT AND URGENT QUESTION IS, 'WHAT ARE YOU DOING
FOR OTHERS?'

The man that many hold as the greatest mind of our times, Albert Einstein, said this:

ONLY A LIFE LIVED FOR OTHERS IS WORTHWHILE.

A HUNDRED TIMES EVERY DAY I REMIND MYSELF THAT MY INNER AND OUTER LIFE DEPEND ON THE LABORS OF OTHER MEN, LIVING AND DEAD, AND THAT I MUST EXERT MYSELF IN ORDER TO GIVE IN THE SAME MEASURE AS I HAVE RECEIVED AND AM STILL RECEIVING.

I want to thank all the families and volunteers who have helped us today. Let us not wait for another day of peril, to remember and act on, what we can mean – and must mean – to one another.

The 9/11 National Day of Service and Remembrance was created as part of the Edward M. Kennedy Serve America Act – legislation named for the man who helped bring it into existence. To his last day, Ted Kennedy devoted his life to serving the country he loved, and understood that each person can make a huge difference in this world.

He liked to tell this story:

AN OLD MAN WALKING ALONG A BEACH SAW A YOUNG MAN PICKING UP A STARFISH AND THROWING IT OUT TO SEA. "WHY ARE YOU DOING THAT?" THE OLD MAN ASKED.

THE YOUNG MAN EXPLAINED THAT THE STARFISH HAD BEEN STRANDED ON THE BEACH BY A RECEDING TIDE, AND COULD DIE IN THE DAYTIME SUN. "BUT THE BEACH GOES ON FOR MILES," THE OLD MAN SAID. "AND THERE ARE SO MANY. HOW CAN YOUR EFFORT MAKE ANY DIFFERENCE?"

WITHOUT HESITATION, THE YOUNG MAN THREW ANOTHER STARFISH BACK TO SAFETY IN THE SEA. HE LOOKED AT THE OLD MAN, SMILED, AND SAID: "IT WILL MAKE A DIFFERENCE TO THAT ONE."

Thank you for being with us today.

2010
**REBUILDING**

Once again we meet to commemorate the day that we have come to call 9/11. We have returned to this sacred site to join our hearts together with the names of those we loved and lost.

No other public tragedy has cut our city so deeply. No other place is as filled with our compassion, our love, and our solidarity. It is with the strength of these emotions, as well as the concrete, glass, and steel that is brought in day by day, that we will build on the footprints of the past the foundation of the future.

At this time, please join us and all New Yorkers in a moment of silence.

..............................

It was once impossible to believe that two soaring towers of people and possibilities could be so coldly silenced. Throughout the years, we have sought consolation in what we have learned: that those we lost live on in our memory, and that a measure of grace can be found in the determination to take up the life before us.

The poet Archibald MacLeish wrote:

EVEN AMONG THE RUINS SHALL BEGIN THE WORK,
LARGE IN THE LEVEL MORNING OF THE LIGHT...

...

ONE MAN IN THE SUN ALONE
WALKS BETWEEN THE SILENCE AND THE STONE...

Mayor Bloomberg

MOM WAS FUN AND FAIR

My mother, Ann, worked on the 92nd floor of Tower Two.

I come from a great big crazy Irish family. And my mother was the craziest of us all. She was also the glue that kept us together. She was an incredible sports-woman and a very strong advocate of women athletes. She was opinionated and noisy and fun and competitive and always – always – fair. Sportsmanship, she said, is what sports – and life – are all about.

A young woman she once coached wrote me this: "Your mother inspired me to be the best athlete I could be. She influenced me to continue my athletics by giving me confidence in myself at a very young age."

For work, my mother often had to be out on the road. And when she could, she'd be on the golf course, or watching my kids at a game. But, as fate would have it, nine years ago she was at her desk. Maybe another day she wouldn't have been.

Every year since 2003, I have given out a sportsmanship award at my children's school to an eighth grade girl who most embodies a drive for excellence, coupled with grace and sportsmanship.

And what I realized is that what I am describing is my mom. My family and I hope that her spirit, crazy and wonderful and full of fairness, will live on and on.

Godspeed Mom, you're always in our thoughts and prayers.

Both grief and celebration are ancient emotions. To accept both is to learn how to embrace the task and the life before us. We have learned, inch by inch, that the best way through the dark nights of our personal sorrow is to link our hands with those who can lead us toward the daybreak of a new day.

Today, as in years past, the names of those who died will be read by their families. This year, they will be joined by those who work daily at this site, who labor with their hands, their sweat, and their imagination.

As the American poet Matthew Shenoda wrote:

INGENUITY IS THE NOTION OF BUILDING
ON A FOUNDATION MADE FROM LOSS

THE BUILDERS (excerpt)

We come not to mourn, but to remember and rebuild. In the words of Henry Wadsworth Longfellow's poem, "The Builders":

ALL ARE ARCHITECTS OF FATE,
  WORKING IN THESE WALLS OF TIME;
SOME WITH MASSIVE DEEDS AND GREAT,
  SOME WITH ORNAMENTS OF RHYME.

NOTHING USELESS IS, OR LOW;
  EACH THING IN ITS PLACE IS BEST;
AND WHAT SEEMS BUT IDLE SHOW
  STRENGTHENS AND SUPPORTS THE REST.

FOR THE STRUCTURE THAT WE RAISE,
  TIME IS WITH MATERIALS FILLED;
OUR TO-DAYS AND YESTERDAYS
  ARE THE BLOCKS WITH WHICH WE BUILD.
        . . .

BUILD TO-DAY, THEN, STRONG AND SURE,
  WITH A FIRM AND AMPLE BASE;
AND ASCENDING AND SECURE
  SHALL TO-MORROW FIND ITS PLACE.

THUS ALONE CAN WE ATTAIN
  TO THOSE TURRETS, WHERE THE EYE
SEES THE WORLD AS ONE VAST PLAIN,
  AND ONE BOUNDLESS REACH OF SKY.

My brother, Christopher Epps, worked for Marsh & McLennan on the
98th floor of Tower One.

I worked across the street from the World Trade Center and when I got to
work that day someone yelled "World Trade Center on fire!" I knew my brother
worked there, so I immediately left work to look for him.

Christopher was the youngest of our parents' seven children. He loved his family
very deeply and would do anything for us. He loved "Star Wars" movies and when
I found out that he was inside the tower that had fallen, I wrote him this poem.

MY BELOVED BROTHER

CHRISTOPHER, CHRISTOPHER SO HANDSOME AND OH SO FINE
WITH A HEART OF GOLD WHY OH WHY DID YOU HAVE TO LEAVE US BEHIND?
AND I SAID TO MYSELF I KNOW WHY
GOD WAS LOOKING FOR A CAPTAIN OF A SHIP,
SOMEONE WHO QUALIFIES AS A JEDI.
SO GO ON DEAR BROTHER DON'T BE SHY,
YOUR SHIP AWAITS YOU WITH TWO THOUSAND AND MORE TO STAND BY YOUR SIDE.
TO TRAVEL WITH YOU ON YOUR JOURNEY INTO THE SKY.
YOUR PANCAKES ARE ON THE GRIDDLE AND THERE'S PLENTY OF SWEET POTATO PIE
OH HOW I WANT TO CRY BECAUSE WHEN GOD HAD CHOSEN YOU HE TRULY CHOSE A JEDI.
MAY THE FORCE BE WITH YOU!

Christopher, we love you and you are embedded in our hearts forever.

Your family.

The American poet who came here from India, Sri Chinmoy, wrote:

HOPE
KNOWS NO FEAR.

HOPE DARES TO BLOSSOM
EVEN INSIDE THE ABYSMAL ABYSS.

HOPE SECRETLY FEEDS
AND STRENGTHENS
PROMISE.

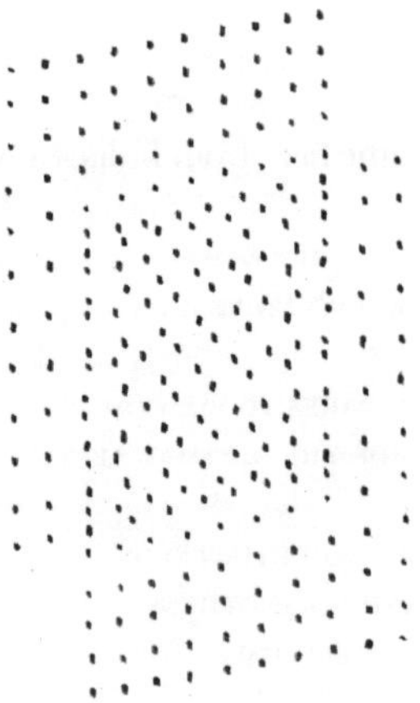

DREAMS

The great poet Langston Hughes told us to:

HOLD FAST TO DREAMS
FOR IF DREAMS DIE
LIFE IS A BROKEN-WINGED BIRD
THAT CANNOT FLY.

HOLD FAST TO DREAMS
FOR WHEN DREAMS GO
LIFE IS A BARREN FIELD
FROZEN WITH SNOW.

IN MY BROTHER'S NAME

I am the brother of New York City Police Officer Glen Pettit, who perished in the South Tower.

Glen had many accomplishments in his short life. He was a volunteer fireman, an avid photographer and videographer, and even received an Emmy award for his work. Glen's true love was being a police officer with his camera on his shoulder. He truly enjoyed helping others and giving to his community.

Let's not remember his life by his accomplishments, but remember him for who he really was, the memories he left in our hearts. What our family will always remember about Glen was his bright blue eyes, his big Irish smile, and his practical jokes.

We will never forget the sacrifice you made that day, with your brothers from Lakeland Fire Department, John Napolitano, Billy Mahoney, James Amato, Peter Brennan, and Chief Larry Stack.

My family started a foundation in my brother's name. With the money we raise for the Glen Pettit Foundation, we are able to give out scholarships to graduating high school seniors who are entering college – to help others just as Glen was always doing.

Glen,

MAY THE SUN SHINE UPON YOUR FACE, MAY THE WIND ALWAYS BE AT YOUR BACK, AND UNTIL WE MEET AGAIN, MAY GOD HOLD YOU IN THE PALM OF HIS HAND.

We love you, we miss you, and we will definitely never forget.

Neil Pettit

ULYSSES (excerpt)

Ulysses was imagined by the poet, as he stood on the highest ground and looked back over his life.

THOUGH MUCH IS TAKEN, MUCH ABIDES; AND THOUGH
WE ARE NOT NOW THAT STRENGTH WHICH IN OLD DAYS
MOVED EARTH AND HEAVEN, THAT WHICH WE ARE, WE ARE,
ONE EQUAL TEMPER OF HEROIC HEARTS,
MADE WEAK BY TIME AND FATE, BUT STRONG IN WILL
TO STRIVE, TO SEEK, TO FIND, AND NOT TO YIELD.

A NATION'S STRENGTH (excerpt)

Ralph Waldo Emerson, the New England philosopher and poet, wrote:

NOT GOLD BUT ONLY MEN CAN MAKE
A PEOPLE GREAT AND STRONG;
MEN WHO FOR TRUTH AND HONOR'S SAKE
STAND FAST AND SUFFER LONG.

BRAVE MEN WHO WORK WHILE OTHERS SLEEP,
WHO DARE WHILE OTHERS FLY...
THEY BUILD A NATION'S PILLARS DEEP
AND LIFT THEM TO THE SKY.

The great American writer Willa Cather wrote:

THE HISTORY OF EVERY COUNTRY BEGINS IN THE HEART OF A MAN OR A WOMAN.

I want to thank each man, woman, and child – both the families and the workers – who have helped us today. It's in your hearts and safekeeping, that not only our past is written, but also our future. For while the heart still aches, tomorrow arrives and we must go to meet it.

One of our best-loved living poets, Dana Gioia, wrote:

WHOEVER YOU ARE: STEP OUT OF DOORS TONIGHT,
OUT OF THE ROOM THAT LETS YOU FEEL SECURE.
INFINITY IS OPEN TO YOUR SIGHT.
WHOEVER YOU ARE.

2011
**THE TENTH ANNIVERSARY**

INTRODUCTION

Ten years have passed since a perfect blue sky morning turned into the blackest of nights. Since then, we have lived in sunshine and in shadow.

And although we can never "unsee" what happened here, we can also see that children who lost their parents have grown into young adults, grandchildren have been born, and good works and public service have taken root to honor those loved and lost.

In all the years that Americans have looked to these ceremonies, we have shared both words and silences. The words of writers and poets have helped express what is in our hearts. The silences have given us a chance to reflect and remember.

And in remembrance of all those who died in New York in 1993 and 2001, at the Pentagon, and near the fields of Shanksville, Pennsylvania, please join us in observing our first moment of silence.

PSALM 46

GOD IS OUR REFUGE AND STRENGTH, A VERY PRESENT HELP IN TROUBLE.
THEREFORE WE WILL NOT FEAR,
EVEN THOUGH THE EARTH BE REMOVED,
AND THOUGH THE MOUNTAINS BE CARRIED INTO THE MIDST OF THE SEA;
THOUGH ITS WATERS ROAR AND BE TROUBLED,
THOUGH THE MOUNTAINS SHAKE WITH ITS SWELLING.
THERE IS A RIVER WHOSE STREAMS SHALL MAKE GLAD THE CITY OF GOD,
THE HOLY PLACE OF THE TABERNACLE OF THE MOST HIGH.
GOD IS IN THE MIDST OF HER, SHE SHALL NOT BE MOVED;
GOD SHALL HELP HER, JUST AT THE BREAK OF DAWN.
THE NATIONS RAGED, THE KINGDOMS WERE MOVED;
HE UTTERED HIS VOICE, THE EARTH MELTED.
THE LORD OF HOSTS IS WITH US;
THE GOD OF JACOB IS OUR REFUGE.
COME, BEHOLD THE WORKS OF THE LORD,
WHO HAS MADE DESOLATIONS IN THE EARTH.
HE MAKES WARS CEASE TO THE END OF THE EARTH;
HE BREAKS THE BOW AND CUTS THE SPEAR IN TWO;
HE BURNS THE CHARIOT IN THE FIRE.
BE STILL, AND KNOW THAT I AM GOD;
I WILL BE EXALTED AMONG THE NATIONS,
I WILL BE EXALTED IN THE EARTH!
THE LORD OF HOSTS IS WITH US;
THE GOD OF JACOB IS OUR REFUGE.

President Obama

They were our neighbors, our friends, our husbands, wives, brothers, sisters, children, and parents. They were the ones who rushed in to help: 2,983 innocent men, women, and children.

We have asked their families to come here, to speak the names out loud, to remind us that each person we lost – in New York, in Washington, and Pennsylvania – had a face, a story, and a life cut out from under them.

As we listen, let us recall the words of Shakespeare:

YOUR CAUSE OF SORROW
MUST NOT BE MEASURED BY HIS WORTH, FOR THEN
IT HATH NO END.

President Lincoln not only understood the heartbreak of his country, he also understood the cost of sacrifice and reached out to console those in sorrow as best he could. In the fall of 1864, he learned that a widow had lost five sons in the Civil War and wrote her this letter:

DEAR MADAM:

I HAVE BEEN SHOWN IN THE FILES OF THE WAR DEPARTMENT A STATEMENT OF THE ADJUTANT GENERAL OF MASSACHUSETTS THAT YOU ARE THE MOTHER OF FIVE SONS WHO HAVE DIED GLORIOUSLY ON THE FIELD OF BATTLE.

I FEEL HOW WEAK AND FRUITLESS MUST BE ANY WORDS OF MINE WHICH SHOULD ATTEMPT TO BEGUILE YOU FROM THE GRIEF OF A LOSS SO OVERWHELMING. BUT I CANNOT REFRAIN FROM TENDERING TO YOU THE CONSOLATION THAT MAY BE FOUND IN THE THANKS OF THE REPUBLIC THEY DIED TO SAVE.

I PRAY THAT OUR HEAVENLY FATHER MAY ASSUAGE THE ANGUISH OF YOUR BEREAVEMENT, AND LEAVE YOU ONLY THE CHERISHED MEMORY OF THE LOVED AND LOST, AND THE SOLEMN PRIDE THAT MUST BE YOURS, TO HAVE LAID SO COSTLY A SACRIFICE UPON THE ALTAR OF FREEDOM.

YOURS, VERY SINCERELY AND RESPECTFULLY,

ABRAHAM LINCOLN

My father, Pete, worked on the 88th floor of the World Trade Center. I was thirteen when I stood here in 2003 and read a poem about how much I just wanted to break down and cry. Since then, I've stopped crying but I've never stopped missing my dad. He was awesome.

My brother, Austin, had just turned two when he passed. I've tried to teach him all the things my father taught me: how catch a baseball, how to ride a bike, and to work hard in school. My dad always said how important it was.

Since 9/11, my mother, brother, and I moved to Florida. I got a job and enrolled in college. I wish my dad had been there – to teach me how to drive, ask a girl out on a date, and see me graduate from high school. And a hundred other things I can't even begin to name.

He worked in an environmental department and cared about the Earth and our future. I know he wanted to make a difference. I admire him for that and would have liked to talk to him about such things. I've decided to become a forensic scientist. I hope that I can make my father proud of the young men my brother and I have become.

I miss you Dad.

TOLLING OF THE BELLS

The poet John Donne wrote:

NEVER SEND TO KNOW FOR WHOM THE BELL TOLLS; IT TOLLS FOR THEE.

This year, we will hear the bells toll six times. To mark the two strikes against the buildings in New York. The fall of the two World Trade Center Towers. The crash of Flight 93 over Pennsylvania. And – now – for the attack on the Pentagon in Washington, DC.

FDR'S FOUR FREEDOMS (excerpt)

As Archibald MacLeish wrote:

THERE ARE THOSE WHO SAY THAT THE FREEDOM OF MAN AND MIND IS NOTHING
BUT A DREAM. THEY ARE RIGHT. IT IS THE AMERICAN DREAM.

In 1941, President Franklin Delano Roosevelt defined for the world the four freedoms on which the American dream is based:

THE FIRST IS FREEDOM OF SPEECH AND EXPRESSION — EVERYWHERE IN THE WORLD.
THE SECOND IS FREEDOM OF EVERY PERSON TO WORSHIP GOD IN HIS OR HER OWN WAY
        — EVERYWHERE IN THE WORLD.
THE THIRD IS FREEDOM FROM WANT — EVERYWHERE IN THE WORLD.
THE FOURTH IS FREEDOM FROM FEAR — ANYWHERE IN THE WORLD.

That is our goal.

OUR STRENGTH IS IN OUR UNITY OF PURPOSE.
TO THAT HIGH CONCEPT, THERE CAN BE NO END SAVE VICTORY.

YOU WILL ALWAYS BE MY HERO

James:
Five years ago, with my daughter, Patricia, at my side, I told you about my wife and Patricia's mother, Police Officer Moira Smith, who ran into the towers time and time again to save as many people as she could. Moira sacrificed all that she had, and all the richness of life that laid before her, in order to save just one more person. Moira was killed when the South Tower collapsed.

Since that time, Patricia has blossomed into a lovely twelve year old, the very picture of her mother, with her mom's smile and sense of adventure.
Our family has grown. Patricia now has two little brothers to share her zest for life. Five years ago we looked back and gave words to our sorrow. Today we choose to remember and share the joy Moira brought to us all, and we vow that she will always live in our hearts.

Patricia:
Mom, I am proud to be your daughter.
You will always be my hero and the pride of New York City.

TURN AGAIN TO LIFE

Today, as you look over the walls of remembrance, we want to share with you the words of the poet Mary Lee Hall who wrote "Turn Again to Life."

IF I SHOULD DIE AND LEAVE YOU HERE A WHILE,
BE NOT LIKE OTHERS SORE UNDONE,
WHO KEEP LONG VIGIL BY THE SILENT DUST.
FOR MY SAKE TURN AGAIN TO LIFE AND SMILE,
NERVING THY HEART AND TREMBLING HAND
TO DO SOMETHING TO COMFORT OTHER HEARTS THAN THINE.
COMPLETE THESE DEAR UNFINISHED TASKS OF MINE
AND I PERCHANCE MAY THEREIN COMFORT YOU.

May God bless those heroes we lost on September 11. The brave men and women who responded so courageously, the heroes we have lost since that day defending our freedom, the men and women today who risk their lives here and abroad to defend our freedom.

No words cried out so fully from the broken heart of our nation as those of a poem called "The Names." It was written by the United States Poet Laureate, Billy Collins, a year after the attacks – and dedicated, simply, to those who died and to their survivors. Its last verse reads:

NAMES ETCHED ON THE HEAD OF A PIN.
ONE NAME SPANNING A BRIDGE, ANOTHER UNDERGOING A TUNNEL.
A BLUE NAME NEEDLED INTO THE SKIN.
NAMES OF CITIZENS, WORKERS, MOTHERS AND FATHERS,
THE BRIGHT-EYED DAUGHTER, THE QUICK SON.
ALPHABET OF NAMES IN A GREEN FIELD.
NAMES IN THE SMALL TRACKS OF BIRDS.
NAMES LIFTED FROM A HAT
OR BALANCED ON THE TIP OF THE TONGUE.
NAMES WHEELED INTO THE DIM WAREHOUSE OF MEMORY.
SO MANY NAMES, THERE IS BARELY ROOM ON THE WALLS OF THE HEART.

ECCLESIASTES

The perspective that we need, and have needed to get through the last ten years and the years that remain, are best expressed in the book of Ecclesiastes:

TO EVERY THING THERE IS A SEASON, AND A TIME FOR EVERY PURPOSE
UNDER HEAVEN:
A TIME TO BE BORN, AND A TIME TO DIE;
A TIME TO PLANT, AND A TIME TO PLUCK UP THAT WHICH HAS PLANTED;
A TIME TO KILL, AND A TIME TO HEAL;
A TIME TO WEEP, AND A TIME TO LAUGH;
A TIME TO MOURN, AND A TIME TO DANCE;
A TIME TO CAST AWAY STONES, AND A TIME TO GATHER STONES TOGETHER;
A TIME TO EMBRACE, AND A TIME TO REFRAIN FROM EMBRACING;
A TIME TO SEEK, AND A TIME TO LOSE;
A TIME TO KEEP, AND A TIME TO CAST AWAY;
A TIME TO REND, AND A TIME TO SEW;
A TIME TO KEEP SILENCE, AND A TIME TO SPEAK;
A TIME TO LOVE, AND A TIME TO HATE;
A TIME OF WAR, AND A TIME OF PEACE.

God bless every soul that we lost. God bless the family members who have to endure that loss. And God, guide us to our reunion in heaven.

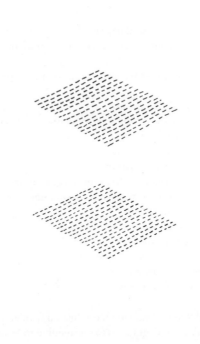

TO SEE HIS NAME ENGRAVED

It has been ten years and it feels like it just happened yesterday. My brother, Christopher Epps, worked on the 98th floor of the North Tower, and not one holiday or birthday goes by that my four sisters and brother and I don't think about him. Our mother never takes off the necklace with his picture in it.

Something I have learned in these past ten years is that people come forward to help you in your hour of need. And today we thank you. The people of our great nation, our family, friends, and neighbors.

At work, Christopher sat next to his good friend Wayne Russo. The Russo family made a special request that their son's name be put next to my brother's name on the memorial wall. That has meant so much to our family.

What I understand now is that the "forces of good" are not just in movies, but all around us. People really do reach out to catch you when you fall. It has been a blessing. Christopher would have loved knowing that the love he gave so freely to others has been given back to us in his name.

Debra Epps

A POEM SAVED

There was a family room just across the way, where families and friends came to write their thoughts or leave a photo and sign their name. A woman who lost her son wrote beside his picture:

TO THE WORLD HE MAY HAVE BEEN JUST ONE PERSON, BUT TO ME, HE WAS THE WORLD.

A father wrote this poem in the scrapbook, and inscribed it to his daughter:

IF TEARS COULD BRING YOU BACK TO ME,
YOU'D BE HERE BY MY SIDE
FOR GOD COULD FILL A RIVER FULL
WITH ALL THE TEARS I'VE CRIED.
IF I COULD HAVE ONE WISH COME TRUE,
I'D ASK OF GOD IN PRAYER
TO LET ME HAVE JUST ONE MORE DAY
TO SHOW HOW MUCH I CARE.
IF LOVE COULD REACH TO HEAVEN'S SHORE,
I'D QUICKLY COME FOR YOU.
MY HEART WOULD BUILD A BRIDGE OF LOVE,
ONE WIDE ENOUGH FOR TWO.

CLOSING

Thank you all for helping us mark this tenth anniversary. The 9/11 Memorial, which opens today, is built as a place where we can touch the face of history and the names of all those we lost. We also remember that out of a day of unspeakable horror, came an endless outpouring of human kindness that reaffirmed our connection to one another. It will guide us as we go forward.

The great American writer James Baldwin wrote:

GENERATIONS DO NOT CEASE TO BE BORN...AND WE ARE RESPONSIBLE TO THEM BECAUSE WE ARE THE ONLY WITNESSES THEY HAVE. THE SEA RISES, THE LIGHT FAILS, LOVERS CLING TO EACH OTHER, AND CHILDREN CLING TO US. THE MOMENT WE CEASE TO HOLD EACH OTHER, THE MOMENT WE BREAK FAITH WITH ONE ANOTHER, THE SEA ENGULFS US AND THE LIGHT GOES OUT.

Mayor Bloomberg

**ACKNOWLEDGMENTS**

2002

Gettysburg Address by President Abraham Lincoln
"I give you this one thought to keep" Native American prayer
The Declaration of Independence

2003

"Stars" by Deborah Chandra
"The Names" by Billy Collins
"I Think Continually of Those Who Were Truly Great" by Stephen Spender
*You Learn by Living* by Eleanor Roosevelt
"A Little Girl's Poem" by Gwendolyn Brooks
Selected quotes by Winston Churchill

2004

The second book of Samuel
Letter to Mrs. Bixby from President Abraham Lincoln

2005

*The People, Yes* by Carl Sandburg
"Remember" by Christina Rossetti
"Letter" by Katherine Mansfield
"For a Reason" by Jean Norris
"The Well Dressed Man with a Beard" by Wallace Stevens

2006

"How Deep Is The Ocean (How High Is The Sky)" by Irving Berlin
"And Not My Wounds" by Mark Van Doren
"Dirge Without Music" by Edna St. Vincent Millay
"What Is Success" by Bessie Stanley
"Turn Again to Life" by Mary Lee Hall
*Macbeth* by William Shakespeare

2007

"On Anothers Sorrow" by William Blake
"Meditation XVII" by John Donne
Selected quotes by Elie Wiesel
"Nothing Personal" by James Baldwin
"Katrina's Sun-Dial" by Henry Van Dyke
*The Madwoman of Chaillot* by Jean Giraudoux

2008

"Losing a Loved One" by Albert Camus
"Try to Praise the Mutilated World" by Adam Zagajewski
"For The Fallen" by Laurence Binyon
*Agamemnon* by Aeschylus
"The Guest House" by Rumi
"Reality Demands" by Wislawa Szymborska
"The Peace of Wild Things" by Wendell Berry

2009

"Wild Geese" by Mary Oliver
"i carry your heart with me(i carry it in" by E.E. Cummings
"I Dream'd in a Dream" by Walt Whitman
"If I can stop one Heart from breaking" by Emily Dickinson
Selected quotes by Martin Luther King, Jr.
"The World As I See It" by Albert Einstein

2010

"The Sheep in the Ruins" by Archibald MacLeish
"Donkey Carts and Desolation" by Matthew Shenoda
"The Builders" by Henry Wadsworth Longfellow
"Hope Knows No Fear" by Sri Chinmoy
"Dreams" by Langston Hughes
"Ulysses" by Alfred, Lord Tennyson
"A Nation's Strength" by Ralph Waldo Emerson
*O Pioneers!* by Willa Cather
"Entrance" by Dana Gioia

2011

Psalm 46
*Macbeth* by William Shakespeare
Letter to Mrs. Bixby from President Abraham Lincoln
"Meditation XVII" by John Donne
Selected quotes by Archibald MacLeish
Four Freedoms by President Franklin Delano Roosevelt
"Turn Again to Life" by Mary Lee Hall
"The Names" by Billy Collins
The book of Ecclesiastes
"Nothing Personal" by James Baldwin

PUBLIC OFFICIALS

Joseph R. Biden,
Vice President of the United States, 2009-

Michael R. Bloomberg,
Mayor of the City of New York, 2002-

George W. Bush,
President of the United States, 2001-2009

Michael Chertoff,
Secretary of Homeland Security of the
United States, 2005-2009

Chris Christie,
Governor of New Jersey, 2010-

Richard J. Codey,
Governor of New Jersey, 2004-2006

Jon S. Corzine,
Governor of New Jersey, 2006-2010

Andrew M. Cuomo,
Governor of New York, 2011-

Donald T. DiFrancesco,
Governor of New Jersey, 2001-2002

Rudolph W. Giuliani,
Mayor of the City of New York, 1994-2001

James E. McGreevey,
Governor of New Jersey, 2002-2004

Barack H. Obama,
President of the United States, 2009-

George E. Pataki,
Governor of New York, 1995-2006

David A. Paterson,
Governor of New York, 2008-2010

Condoleezza Rice,
Secretary of State of the United States,
2005-2009

Eliot L. Spitzer,
Governor of New York, 2007-2008

FAMILY MEMBERS

Grace F. Alviar, 2009

Carolyn Staub Bilelis, 2008

Nancy Brandemarti, 2004

Chris Burke, 2005

Nicholas Chirls, 2007

Sydney R. Chirls, 2007

Brittany Clark, 2002

Benito Colon, 2007

Margaret Cruz, 2006

Charlene Cumberbatch, 2007

Debra J. Epps, 2010, 2011

Kathleen M. Froehner, 2003

K.C. Gross, 2009

Catherine Hernandez, 2008

Kyra Houston, 2005

Anthoula Katsimatides, 2005

Marianne Keane, 2002

Mike Low, 2004

Pearl Maynard, 2004

Larry McGovern, 2010

Joan Molinaro, 2003

Peter W. Negron, 2003, 2011

Neil E. Pettit, 2010

Aidan Salamone, 2008

Alexander Salamone, 2008

Anna Salamone, 2008

Susan Sliwak, 2006

James J. Smith, 2006, 2011

Patricia M. Smith, 2011

Jay S. Winuk, 2009

JAMES AND PATRICIA SMITH, 2006

Amazing Grace
Bach Cello Suite No.1 Sarabande
Beethoven Serenade For Violin,
  Viola and Cello, Op. 8
Borrowed Angels
Bridge Over Troubled Water
Close Your Eyes
Danny Boy
Hero
I Will Remember You
Keep Me In Your Heart
Let the River Run
Over In the Glory Land
The Prayer
Shed a Little Light
Somewhere
The Sound of Silence
Star Spangled Banner
Taps
There You Are Again
Vivaldi Violin Concerto in A Minor,
  Adagio
You Raise Me Up

MUSICIANS

Bloomingdale School
Bronx Arts Ensemble
Brooklyn Philharmonic
Brooklyn Youth Chorus
Molly Carr
Roseanne Cash
Chamber Music Society of
  Lincoln Center
Kristin Chenoweth
Curtis High School
Diller-Quaille School
Emi Ferguson
James Grasek
Harlem School of the Arts

Sharon Isbin
The Juilliard Quartet
The Juilliard School
Harriet Langley
John Leventhal
Lucy Moses School
Yo-Yo Ma
Manhattan School of Music
Wynton Marsalis
Momenta Quartet
Musica de Camara
Musica Reginae
New York Youth Symphony
Orchestra of St. Luke's
Orchestra of the Bronx
Orpheus Chamber Orchestra
Itzhak Perlman
Ben Pila
Queens Symphony
Quintet of the Americas
Riverside Symphony
Paula Robison
Gil Shaham
Carly Simon
Paul Simon
Songs of Solomon
St. Paul's String Quartet
Staten Island Chamber Music Players
Benjamin Taylor
James Taylor
Kate Taylor
Livingston Taylor
Sally Taylor
Third Street Music School
Emily Thomas
Young People's Chorus of New York City
Hung Wen Yu
Fred Zlotkin

THE FIRST CEREMONY, 2002

SOUTH MEMORIAL POOL, 2011

TENTH ANNIVERSARY, 2011

Despite their size and stature, the 9/11 ceremonies always felt deeply personal.

The honor I felt to be involved, finding readings and working with the families, still fills me with gratitude, a chance to play a small part in these moving September mornings. The families who spoke, brave souls who were neither public speakers nor writers, began with hope and trepidation. What a privilege to be let into their lives and deepest of feelings. I thank them for their stories, and willingness to speak from the heart.

Looking back at what was read over the ten years, we all saw a chance to create a record and a keepsake, a book of love and consolation. I want to start by thanking New York City's First Deputy Mayor Patricia E. Harris for her encouragement and sensitivity every step of the way.

Martha Kaplan, our invaluable book agent, believed in the project and found it the right home; great thanks to Craig Cohen at powerHouse Books. Designer Carin Goldberg beautifully transformed not just words but feelings into print. Kate Levin, New York City's Commissioner of Cultural Affairs, was a guiding spirit from the moment the idea of readings began. Lynn Rasic, at the National September 11 Memorial & Museum, became a champion of the book, a partner in its completion, along with Allie Skayne. Nancy Cutler in the Mayor's Office, our steady hands-on, moved things forward so the book was published with elegance and integrity.

A book like this truly begins in the hearts of all those who helped make the 9/11 ceremonies so delicately powerful. Without the talents and imagination of Don Mischer and his caring team, Christy Ferer's work as liaison with the families, all the musicians and thousands of readers, and the hard work of every government agency involved, none of the great hopes for the ceremonies could have become a reality. Every year you felt the good will, concern, late nights, and early mornings of hundreds of people, from top management to volunteers, acting together for something larger than themselves. And heartfelt thanks for the ongoing work of the Board of the 9/11 Memorial, its president Joe Daniels, and his dedicated staff.

Finally, our gratitude to all the poets, authors, and families who gave us permission to reprint their words. They lent grace to a day filled with grief, gave us the words to express the incomprehensible, and the companionship of understanding that lets the light into an endless night.

Sara Lukinson

September Morning:
Ten Years of Poems and Readings from the 9/11 Ceremonies New York City

Editing and Compilation © National September 11 Memorial and Museum at the World Trade Center
Foundation, Inc.

Photographs:
"James and Patricia Smith, 2006" © 2012, The City of New York, all rights reserved. Photograph by Frank Daum.
"The First Ceremony, 2002" © 2012, The City of New York, all rights reserved. Photograph by Joseph Reyes.
"South Memorial Pool, 2011" © 2012, 9/11 Memorial. Photograph by Amy Dreher.
"Tenth Anniversary, 2011" © 2012, 9/11 Memorial. Photograph by Jin Lee.
"Names on the Memorial, 2011" © 2012, 9/11 Memorial. Photograph by Jin Lee.

Illustrations © 2012, Brian Rea

Published in the United States by powerHouse Books,
a division of powerHouse Cultural Entertainment, Inc.
37 Main Street, Brooklyn, NY 11201-1021
telephone 212.604.9074, fax 212.366.5247
e-mail: septembermorning@powerhousebooks.com
website: www.powerhousebooks.com

First edition, 2012

Library of Congress Control Number: 2012938161

ISBN 978-1-57687-618-3

Compiled and Edited by Sara Lukinson
Illustrations: Brian Rea
Cover and Book Design: Carin Goldberg Design
Assistant Designer: Pablo Delkan
Coordinator: Suzanne Holt

A complete catalog of powerHouse Books and Limited Editions is available upon request; please call, write,
or visit our website.

10 9 8 7 6 5 4 3 2 1

Printed and bound in China through Asia Pacific Offset

NAMES ON THE MEMORIAL, 2011